PRAISE FOR *TO FEEL THE MUSIC*

"*To Feel the Music* is a fascinating tale about countless intersections: of artistry and technology, of creativity and commerce, of entrepreneurs and organizers, of the individual and the team. It's heartbreaking on some fronts and inspiring in many others. I will never listen to music in quite the same way after reading this book, nor ever again take for granted the ingenuity behind the high-tech devices amid which we live."

—James Fallows, national correspondent, *The Atlantic*

"One of the greatest musicians of all time, Neil Young knows the effort artists put into their work so that their audiences can feel the music. In a very easy-to-understand way, Neil explains how, unlike for photographs or television, each generation of digital technology has further degraded sound quality. Neil and collaborator Phil Baker lay out concrete solutions to restore music fidelity without sacrificing listener convenience in this fascinating read brimming with passion."

—Dan Hesse, retired CEO, Sprint

"This book provides backstage access to a fascinating story about the intersection of art, technology, and business. Young and Baker's passion for their respective crafts is tangible on every page."

—Harry McCracken, technology editor, *Fast Company*

"Neil Young is not only a rock star in the music industry. He has emerged as a rock star in championing and challenging the tech industry to deliver the kind of sound quality that he and other musicians want their audiences to experience as they do when they record their music . . . The book is a call to action for the tech industry to strive to deliver the best audio quality possible, so that those who listen to Neil Young's songs and music, as well as those from other artists, experience exactly what the artists hear when they create their music."

—Tim Bajarin, president, Creative Strategies, Inc.

"The alchemy of product development is rarely shared like this, from a music legend (and it turns out, an enlightened CEO) and a tech veteran, with refreshing candor about the highs and lows of bringing together people, materials, and energy to deliver sound as intended, straight to the soul."

—Louis Kim, vice president, Hewlett-Packard

to Feel the Music

to Feel the Music

A SONGWRITER'S MISSION TO SAVE HIGH-QUALITY AUDIO

NEIL YOUNG AND PHIL BAKER

BenBella Books, Inc.
Dallas, TX

BenBella Books, Inc.
10440 N. Central Expressway, Suite 800
Dallas, TX 75231
www.benbellabooks.com
Send feedback to feedback@benbellabooks.com

Printed in the United States of America
10 9 8 7 6 5 4 3 2 1

Library of Congress Cataloging-in-Publication Control Number: 2019010120.
ISBN 9781948836388 (trade cloth)
ISBN 9781948836630 (electronic)

Copyediting by James Fraleigh
Proofreading by Michael Fedison and Cape Cod Compositors, Inc.
Text design by Aaron Edmiston
Cover design by Marc Whitaker / MTWdesign.net
Illustrations in chapters 2 and 3 by Kenshi Sakurai for Toshi Onuki Studio
Insert design by Toshi Onuki Studio
Printed by Lake Book Manufacturing

Distributed to the trade by Two Rivers Distribution, an Ingram brand
www.tworiversdistribution.com

Special discounts for bulk sales are available.
Please contact bulkorders@benbellabooks.com.

To my wife, Daryl, for her artistry and her support of mine. To John Hanlon, my co-producer, and Tim Mulligan, my longtime engineer, for their great work to ensure my music is of the highest technical quality; and to all the people who love my music, you have made my life so full!

And to the late Elliot Roberts, my best friend and manager, who tirelessly supported improving audio quality in his life, knowing that to feel the music, you had to hear as much of it as possible. Elliot understood the urgency of saving an art form for posterity, saving the history of music in its highest quality. Thanks Elliot, for all you have done.

—NEIL YOUNG

To my wife, Jane, for her love and support for over fifty years. To my daughter, Karen; son, Dan; daughter-in-law, Holly; and grandsons, Kyan and Clive, for their love, their humor, and for bringing so much joy to my life.

And with great thanks to Neil for entrusting me to help implement his vision for preserving the highest quality of recorded music.

—PHIL BAKER

Contents

A Message from Neil

I'd love for you to experience my high-quality music by visiting www.NeilYoungArchives.com and listening to the album of the week and song of the day.

Introduction

Neil

Musicians such as myself attempt to record music at the highest sound quality available. We take excruciating care to preserve every detail from each instrument, each voice, and the surrounding environment. We do this knowing that the more you hear, the more you feel the music in your soul.

However, today's recording and tech industries just don't care about the sound of music. They're content to deliver music at a much lower quality, essentially stripping and dumbing down the art of recorded music, so that listeners are able to hear only a small part of the original audio recordings. These original recordings can have depth, breadth, and clarity that captures all of the subtleties, echoes, reverberations, and characteristics of the performance environment. The compressed versions, on the other hand, lack all of those details, sounding muddy, one-dimensional, and flat. The decision to compress music not only affects what we hear now—it will affect what we'll be able to hear in the future, too.

To Feel the Music is an account of my efforts to challenge the music industry and the technology community on behalf of all artists and music fans to restore audio quality to what it once was and to save the soul of the music, thereby saving the future of music. This effort to rescue music is the most important professional undertaking of my entire career.

This book chronicles how I and a small team invented and brought to market solutions that serve as an example of what *could* be done. With Pono, my early effort at creating a high-resolution music player and download service, we showed the industry that it was possible to deliver the highest-quality audio to thousands of music lovers at an affordable cost. What we did was not anything extraordinary. Others in the industry could have done it, though few seemed to care. But that was not the end of our efforts; it was just the beginning.

As music streaming increased, the industry moved to even poorer-quality audio. The sound of music went from bad to worse. Yet, I was convinced there must be a solution. If streaming was the future, couldn't it be better? To that end, I worked with an even smaller team, including a tiny company in Singapore called OraStream, and we developed new streaming technology that is far superior to anything else available. I've introduced this high-resolution streaming on my Neil Young Archives (NYA). Called Xstream by NYA, it was my follow-up to Pono, to marry the convenience of streaming with the best quality that users' devices can handle. High-res streaming is my second initiative to show the industry what can be done.

I've put my name and reputation on the cause of better audio. I've pointed out the failures of the tech giants to deliver it and will continue to do so because it's something I believe in very deeply. I'm going to continue this quest on behalf of musicians and music lovers so that all of you can hear what you deserve—just what was intended by the artists who created it.

Phil

I first met Neil in 2012 when he asked me to help him develop a new music player. I encountered not just the famous musician whose work is legendary, but also someone who had a passionate mission extending back decades to save music. He wanted to restore what had been missing since the invention of the CD: high-quality audio. Throughout all these years his mission hasn't changed. It was his passion before I met him, and it continues to be his passion now.

I had the luck and opportunity to make a small contribution through the development of the Pono music player, a simple-to-use, low-cost device that delivered music of unparalleled clarity. And, more recently, I've worked with Neil to help develop the NYA website and apps, which delivers the music as well as Pono does, using an innovative streaming technology.

I was able to see how important high-quality audio is to Neil and how all-consuming his goal was. It is completely altruistic on Neil's part, not motivated by making money, certainly not for fame. While some critics have had trouble understanding this or have questioned his motives, I have been there for all the discussions and the meetings, and I want to help tell the real story.

While visiting the Musician's Hall of Fame in Nashville, I was struck by how much effort has been put into perfecting the recording and playback of music over the past century to bring audio of the best possible quality to those who could not be present at a live performance. From the gramophone to the radio to reel-to-reel tape recorders to the tape cassette to huge speakers and amplifiers, each invention was about creating a faithful reproduction of the original. Yet modern technology has taken us in a different direction, replacing quality with convenience. The long history of these efforts that I saw on display in the museum suddenly came to a stop and began to reverse course.

Although I'm not a musician, I have a background and career in technology, so this regression really hit home. Technology, which we think of as improving our lives, was failing music lovers. This put into perspective what Neil, I, and the rest of the team had been doing.

To Feel the Music is also about what it takes for a small company to begin with an idea and turn it into a product. It's the story of a technology startup business with grand ambitions but limited resources and the challenges it faced trying to turn Neil's vision into reality. It takes the reader through the numerous steps required to develop, manufacture, and sell a consumer hardware product.

I try to expose the product development process, with all the imperfections and unexpected challenges that befall most products. It's a process that depends on a group of people from diverse backgrounds coming together and working as a team, often with conflicting goals and ideas. It shows how the product idea is often the easiest part, and how complex and unexpected the implementation can be. And then when the product is done, what is its measure of success? Is it a product that performs as it was envisioned, one that can be manufactured inexpensively, or one that's successful in the market? *To Feel the Music* takes you into all of these areas that rarely are written about.

Chapter 1 | Neil

THE MOST IMPORTANT
THING I'VE EVER DONE

usic has been one of the great joys of my life. I've performed for more than fifty years and written and recorded
scores of albums. I've traveled around the world per-
forming for audiences in dozens of countries. There's nothing as
good as a live performance where the music is unfiltered—where
it fills the air, reverberates, and is just so pure and organic. Likewise, a great recording that tries to replicate this is also in a class
by itself. It's an art form.

In the sixties and seventies, advances in audio equipment, high-
quality vinyl, and tape recording brought wonderful-sounding
music into the home. While not the same as live performances,
the sound was an art form unto itself and allowed listeners to
enjoy the music, become immersed in it, and be exposed to many
of its nuances.

ENTER THE DIGITAL AGE

Yet in the early eighties, instead of audio improving even more, something unexpected occurred. When digital music became available on the compact disc (CD), I got very excited. I thought, *Finally, no more cracks, no more pops, no more surface noises that had accompanied vinyl records*. All the artifacts would be gone.

When I went into the studio after making my recordings, I did what I usually did. I cranked up the volume and started mixing, listening to CD quality from my new digital machines. After three hours, my ears were killing me! They were ringing and really hurting badly. That was when I first realized that something was wrong.

The CD was a brand-new format, and because it was new, it was highly promoted and pushed very hard by the music and tech industries. But convenient as it was, it was inferior to its predecessors, such as vinyl and tape recordings, in terms of audio quality.

That was the beginning of a downward spiral, where at each step along the way of supposed progress, quality was compromised for convenience. And from that point to today, we've experienced this degradation over and over: multiple new formats, each sounding worse than what came before.

To me it simply made no sense. People tend to dislike new formats since they need to keep buying the same content over and over. But to buy the same content and get something worse? That was terrible! I thought, all we really need is one format, and if we have just one format, it should be great—the best it can be.

Unfortunately, today there is no convenient way for the mass audience to purchase the early high-quality recordings that come close to the original performances. Listeners cannot enjoy the history of recorded sound and the magical recordings of the last century at their finest. These high-quality recordings are currently only available to the elite few who pay a premium for their music and have the expensive equipment needed to enjoy it. And because the audience that can afford these recordings is so small, there's only a very limited number of titles available. Instead, the record companies focus on what they can sell: inferior quality made for cell phones.

The acceptance of poor quality ripples throughout the industry and makes it even more difficult to reverse direction. People get used to hearing this poorer quality and many never experience what music could sound like. As the demand for high-quality audio diminishes, hardware companies struggle to survive and artists record at lower quality. When these companies die, there's nothing available to play quality sound. It's a race to the bottom that affects the entire audio industry.

DIGITAL QUALITY IMPROVES—EXCEPT AUDIO

The deterioration of quality is not happening with other digital content—only audio. Digital video and imaging have made amazing progress. Films in the theater and images we take with our cameras—and even our phones—are sharper and clearer than ever. Advances such as image and contrast correction take advantage of digital technologies to increase enjoyment and provide the detail and fine nuances otherwise lost.

Why can't we say the same about audio? To me, something is wrong. As an artist, I want my fans to experience the same quality that I experience in the studio. I want fans of other artists to be able to do the same. In this age of technology, there is nothing standing in the way of this idea—except greed.

Record companies want to charge a lot more to stream high res just because it sounds better. There is no additional cost to *them* to stream high-resolution music. It's only bandwidth. The consumer's bandwidth costs have plummeted. Should it cost more to listen to good-sounding music than it costs to listen to bad-sounding music? Should the cost be borne by the consumer? I have not yet found a satisfactory answer.

If the record companies were to take the price restrictions off the streaming companies and let them stream whatever they could without additional costs, then it would be up to the streaming companies to improve their technology and bring high-quality music into the twenty-first century. I found a way and did that for my music. I stream in high res on my NYA archive site and NYA apps. Streaming companies could do it, too, but they have not. Why is that?

WHY IS SOUND SO BAD TODAY?

Streaming services are built around old limitations from the twentieth century when memory and bandwidth were expensive. Those limitations were major issues when Apple developed the iPod decades ago using expensive hard drives with limited capacity. Low-cost solid-state memory was unavailable, and data traveled at a fraction of today's speeds. All these things are old issues that no longer exist, yet current music formats are still based on them—held prisoner to them. Music is in a cage.

It's the same with the record companies and the files they sell. They charge high prices for high res, which has nothing to do with anything. Restricting audio quality doesn't make sense from a financial standpoint. If you sell a better product, which you already have access to, and it doesn't cost any more to sell it, then why not? Why hold it back and put an inflated price on it so literally no one buys it? What is the advantage to having something if no one can use it? I just don't get that. If these companies went back a little further than the digital past, they would see that they used to charge almost the same for everything: records, cassettes, and tapes. It was all essentially the same price and quality, and that's when people really loved music, because they could hear it and *feel* it. They could feel the soul of the music, and they loved it.

I think if the highest-quality music audio were available at a reasonable price, the streaming companies would stream it, everybody would hear and feel better music, and the world would be a much happier, better place.

One of the arguments the music and technology industries make about their complacency for not improving music quality is that many people can't hear the difference anyway, so why bother? Well, my response is simple. It doesn't matter if every person can hear the difference or not. Some can, and some can't. If it costs the same amount, what's the big deal?

Look, I know music, I know sound, and I can hear and feel it! There are a lot of color-blind people out there, like myself, but you don't see television sets that don't have color. They didn't take the color out of TV because some people can't see all the colors of the spectrum. They used to say that the limit of TV quality that people could perceive was 2,000 lines of resolution. Yet now manufacturers are introducing sets with 8,000 lines, because some can appreciate the improvement.

I think it's the same thing with tone deafness. If you can't hear the music—the difference in audio quality—it doesn't mean it shouldn't be there. People who can hear it deserve to be able to hear it. Plus, how are others going to find out whether they can hear it? How do they know they can't hear it? What do they have to compare it to? They've been so conditioned to hearing low-quality audio, that's all they hear. They never hear high quality, or if they do hear it, it might be for just a few minutes, and in that short time span they may not be able to absorb the difference. It is subtle, but once discovered, it can be life changing.

If people could listen to high-res music all the time, they might just find they enjoy the music a lot more. You have to give your body a chance to absorb it and recognize how good it feels to hear it. The human body is incredible. It's great! It has such deep sensitivity. It's made by God/nature, depending on your beliefs. If some listeners can hear and feel the input from everywhere, why give them less? There's no advantage. Sticking to lower quality means that all of the people who are sensitive and can hear the quality don't receive it. There's no logical reason to not provide the best and improve the quality of life. That, after all, is one of the goals of technology—to improve our lives.

Music is my life, and it's too important. I want to ensure it is preserved in its highest quality. Sometimes I think, *This could be the most important thing I've ever tried to do.* I don't know if I will succeed at it. But if I do, it will be a great accomplishment, because it affects all the music of all musicians, every recording ever made back to the beginning, not just mine.

So, I am not giving up, because somebody's got to listen to this. Somebody's got to care.

Restoring high-quality audio has been my long-term goal, a much longer term than I thought it would be. We are up against many challenges to make it happen, but we will continue to come up with new ways to succeed.

Chapter 2 | Phil

A LOOK AT AUDIO QUALITY

To better understand what's happened to music, it's useful to understand some of the technology of digital music, the various formats, and some of the forces that shaped their development.

DEFINITIONS

First, high-res digital music, a somewhat vague term, is simply digital music files that have audio quality better than CDs. While it can't always match the original performance in all respects, it does a better job than CDs in providing more of the details and nuances of what was originally recorded.

Audio recordings come in two formats, analog and digital. Analog is made up of a continuous data stream that comes closest to the original sound, since the original sound is analog. Digital audio is a series of discrete, discontinuous data that tries to replicate or simulate the original analog recording.

LIMITATIONS

Analog vs. Digital

With analog audio recordings, such as what's recorded on vinyl and tape, the limitation of the audio quality is often the recording medium itself, which imposes some characteristics on top of the recorded performance; artifacts such as hisses or crackles, for example, may show up as background noise on the recording. The original recording is essentially all there but sometimes slightly impacted by these background effects. Analog quality is dependent on how well the performance can be recorded and how minimal these artifacts are, mostly a function of the recording equipment.

SAMPLING RATE

In contrast, digital audio is "manufactured" from the original performance. The original recording is chopped up into pieces of data (sampled) to represent the recording. How often it takes these samples, and how precise the samples are, affects the sound quality. The more frequent the sampling, the higher the quality; the less frequent, the poorer the representation of the original recording.

How often the analog music is sampled is measured in number of times per second, referred to as frequency. The highest-used sampling rates for music are 384,000 and 192,000 times per second. The unit of measure for frequency is hertz (Hz). A rate of 192,000 times per second or 192 kilohertz (kHz) is considered sufficiently high for essentially all recording needs.

Sampling music is much like sampling a moving object to create a video or movie; the higher the sampling rate the better the representation. Images in old-fashioned movies flickered and were jumpy because the sampling rate was just a few frames per second (fps). With digital cinema, HD video, and Blu-ray, sampling is up to 60 fps, resulting in a smoother and much higher quality representation of the original.

PRECISION AND DEPTH

In addition to the sampling frequency, there is the level of detail, precision, or resolution of each individual sample (just as the number pi can be described as 3.14 or 3.14159265359, low precision and high precision). In audio, it's either a number with 16 or 24 bits of precision, where the latter is better because it's a more precise number. In audio, that precision determines the dynamic range or the accuracy of the sound reproduction. A precision of 24 bits provides a much bigger range in volume or dynamic range (16,777,216 levels compared to 65,536 levels for 16 bits). With more precision, it can also better match the studio's analog performance and capture more of the nuances.

DIGITAL AUDIO QUALITY IN TWO NUMBERS

Digital audio can also be compared to a digital camera that captures an analog scene, which is made up of a continuous series of colors and light levels, by creating pixels. The pixels are samples representative of the color and brightness of tiny areas in the scene. The more pixels (frequency), and the more colors and light levels (bit depth) for each pixel, the more faithfully the digital photo matches the original scene. Likewise, audio quality is defined by a pair of numbers: sampling rate and bit depth.

As noted, the audio industry defines high res as music that is better in quality than CD quality, which is 44.1 kHz with 16 bits of precision, abbreviated as 44.1/16. According to the Recording Industry Association of America's (RIAA's) official definition:

> *High-resolution audio is lossless audio that is capable of reproducing the full range of sound from recordings that have been mastered from better than CD quality music sources.*[1]

Thus, a digital recording made as a 192 kHz/24 bit file is considered to be essentially as a good as a digital file can be. To put all

---

1   RIAA, "High Resolution Audio Initiative Gets Major Boost with New 'Hi-Res MUSIC' Logo and Branding Materials for Digital Retailers," *RIAA News*, June 23, 2015, https://www.riaa.com/high-resolution-audio-initiative-gets-major-boost-with -new-hi-res-music-logo-and-branding-materials-for-digital-retailers/.

of this in perspective, a high-quality analog recording beats a top digital version even if the digital is at 192/24, which is much better than CD quality, which in turn is much better than MP3.

When the original recording is compressed to CD or MP3 levels, the intent is to discard the less important data rather than discarding data randomly. The compression algorithms use a set of rules that might discard the softer passages when there's louder music playing and discard more of the sound occurring in areas where our hearing is less sensitive. But they do discard data that you can hear and feel.

STREAMING NUMBERS

If you are wondering what the corresponding pair of numbers are for low-res streaming, there are none. Streaming uses a different measurement that relates to how many total bits of data are streamed per second. It varies from as little as 24 kbps (thousands of bits per second) to about 320 kbps. With most streaming services, it's 128 or 256 kbps.

High-res music, when expressed using the same units as streaming music, would be 9,216 kbps. (Note: For high-res 192/24 music, 24 bits are sampled 192,000 times per second, so the total data rate is $24 \times 192,000 = 4,608,000$ bits per second = 4,608 kbps of data for each of the two stereo channels, or a total of 9,216 kbps.)

There is a technique to reduce the file size by about 40 percent using an industry lossless compression scheme called FLAC (Free Lossless Audio Codec), so the net result is about 6,000 kbps. This is the amount needed to stream high-res, no-compromised

Audio bit rate comparison

MP3 ♩ **256**kbps

CD ♩♩♩♩ **1,411**kbps

Hi-Res
24-bit/96kHz ♩♩♩♩♩♩♩♩♩♩♩♩♩♩ **6,000**kbps

two-channel audio. That number, 6,000, will vary somewhat, as different music content compresses differently with FLAC.

Thus, low-res streaming music uses anywhere from 24 kbps to 320 kbps compared to about 6,000 kbps for high-res audio and 1,411 kbps for CD quality.

Up to this point we've discussed the quality of the content of the recorded music. The quality is also dependent on how you listen to it.

While better equipment, such as good headphones or speakers, can provide better sound than lesser equipment, most listening experiences with adequate equipment benefit from better recording quality.

During the development of Pono, we listened to hundreds of combinations of players, headphones, and speakers in the office, at home, in the car, and in our audio room, playing files that spanned the full range of quality. We found that, while even the best equipment can't make a poor audio file sound very good, a high-quality audio file improved the listening experience on most equipment.

That's not all that surprising. If you start with a blurry photograph, you can never make it look sharp, but if you start with a sharp photo, it's sharp whether you view it from afar or up close. The information is in the image file no matter how you view it.

In listening to music, sometimes it may not be obvious how much better a high-resolution file can be. It's also like a photo that way. When viewing an image on your phone, it may look great, but as you zoom in or print it out as an enlargement, the defects become obvious. When listening to music playing in the background, not focusing your mind on the music, all files may sound fine. But "zooming" in to carefully listen to music will reveal significant differences. Zooming in to the music means removing other distractions, concentrating on the music, and listening for an extended period. You need to listen to it, giving the music a chance to permeate, and feel the subtleties as it's playing. Over time lower-quality music becomes tiring, even jarring to the listener, while with higher-quality music you can listen for hours. Making the music the focus will bring out the differences.

There's been a perpetual debate about what some can hear, and others cannot, when it comes to high-res audio, similar to other areas of enjoyment, such as wine and photography. Wine is a subject that brings out a range of strong opinions, from those who are willing to spend a lot of money because they appreciate a great Bordeaux, to those who prefer to enjoy a $10 bottle of red table wine. What the enjoyment of wine and audio have in common is people's passion and strongly held opinions, especially when they can be so wildly different. There's often a lack of respect and even disdain from those who belittle others who appreciate the subtleties of wine or audio and are able to discern the differences.

In the field of photography, digital cameras began to be taken seriously when their sensors were capable of creating an image with three million pixels (three megapixels), matching the resolution of a single frame of 35 mm film. At that point "experts" said you couldn't distinguish images that had more than three million pixels, so don't waste your money. Yet, cameras continued to be developed with even higher-resolution sensors, all the way to more than forty megapixels on some pro cameras and even twelve megapixels on smartphone cameras. It turns out that those extra pixels are not wasted. What you get with these higher-quality sensors is more than just better resolution; there are many more nuances that improve the picture quality, such as a wider dynamic range, better contrast, and more subtleties of color.

The fact is that an audio file with a small amount of data does not have many of the subtleties that a higher-resolution file does, much as some wines do not have all of the nuances of other wines, and a low-res image doesn't capture all the subtleties that a high-res image can.

So just what can you hear with high-resolution audio that you cannot with low resolution? It's the spaciousness, the breadth of the sound field, and the ability to hear and feel a ping of a triangle or a pluck of a guitar string, each with all of its own resonance and harmonics that slowly trail off into silence. Music affects many of our senses: sound waves enter our ears, but they also reach other parts of our body. The subtleties of the audio can even trigger our brain to recall a past event in our lives.

When I brought home the first prototype of the Pono player, I asked my wife, Jane, to listen. For more than twenty years, Jane was a singer in the San Diego Master Chorale, San Diego's foremost choir, which often performs with the San Diego Symphony Orchestra. She's been skeptical of many of the products I've designed in the past, and that makes her a great sounding board. She was eager to listen to Pono, not as an audiophile but as a music lover and a musician. Even I was surprised by her reaction.

As she explained at the time, "When I am onstage during a rehearsal or performance, as I sing my part or listen during orchestral interludes, I can hear the purity of tone of each individual instrument, as well as the overtones of the orchestra that give such richness to the sound. In addition, we often perform in acoustically alive venues, such as symphony halls and cathedrals, where the precision of such works as the Verdi *Requiem* or Bach B Minor Mass are enriched with the reverberation of the acoustics of the hall or cathedral.

"I have never before experienced this quality of sound in a home setting—not even close. However, last night, using the Pono player and your Audeze headphones, I listened to an assortment of choral and orchestral works and some more contemporary songs, such as Roberta Flack singing 'Killing Me Softly.' I was amazed by the purity and fullness of the sound. I was able to place the instruments around me, just like standing up onstage with the orchestra. In the case of Flack, her voice was rich and sonorous and at the same time the instrumental background allowed the overtones to come through, along with just enough reverberation."

I never had such an enthusiastic reaction to the scores of products I've worked on over my career. Jane's conclusion was,

"This is the best thing you've ever worked on and others need to hear it! You need to make it happen."

Still, in the high-tech community, there has been skepticism about the value of high-resolution music, and opinions ranged from "I can't tell the difference" to "Just amazing." Neil had a simple response to all of this: "If someone can't tell the difference, that's okay. They shouldn't waste their money. But they shouldn't prevent those who can appreciate the quality from enjoying it."

There's no question in my mind that high-quality music changes not only the content of what you hear, but also impacts your attitude, your energy, and your happiness. There's something special about music in the way it touches us through so many senses. And there's even scientific evidence to confirm what Neil has known all along.

One example comes from a study by scientists at the University of Helsinki who discovered that listening to classical music actually alters the function of our genes.[2] They reported that it "reduces blood pressure, causes the release of dopamine, and even improves muscle function. But new research has found that music has an even more profound effect on our bodies."

In the study, researchers took blood samples from participants before and after listening to Mozart's Violin Concerto No. 3 in G Major, K. 216. They found that the music directly affects human RNA, suggesting that listening to music has even more surprising benefits than previously thought. It affects the very core of your biological being.[3]

---

2   C. Kanduri et al., "The Effect of Listening to Music on Human Transcriptome," *PeerJ*, March 12, 2015, https://peerj.com/articles/830.

3   Natalie Clarkson, "How Does Listening to Classical Music Affect the Body?" Virgin .com, March 24, 2015, https://www.virgin.com/music/how-does-listening-classical -music-affect-body.

The point is that music comes in a range of quality and can be enjoyed in a range of ways. As a universal language, it brings enjoyment to us, whether we are playing it in the background or are in the center of a theater, hearing a live performance. But for most, high-res music comes closest to replicating the live experience, and there is no reason to settle for less.

Because a high-resolution digital music file contains so much more data than a low-res music file, pioneers of MP3s and portable music players had to address several technical issues. High-res music requires more memory to store and faster wireless networks to transmit the additional data. These limitations—more memory, slow networks, and higher data costs—drove many of the decisions found in today's music services, standards, and formats. They led to highly compressed music that used less data to make it easier to send and store.

As Neil has pointed out, these limitations have been rapidly disappearing. Memory costs have plummeted, moving from large complex disk drives to tiny solid-state memory chips. One megabyte of memory cost $6,480 in 1980, $106 in 1990, $1.56 in 2000, $0.19 in 2010, and less than $.007 in 2019. Memory costs are now just a tiny fraction compared to when the iPod was introduced.[4] Yet, it was the iPod that played a major role in cementing the small size of the music file, and that size has barely changed over the past two decades.

Similar progress has been made with data transmission speeds and data costs. High-speed cellular data speeds have gone from 2 mbps (megabits per second) beginning with 3G technology in

---

4   John C. McCallum, "Memory Prices (1957–2018)," JCMIT.net, December 16, 2018, https://jcmit.net/memoryprice.htm.

Historical Cost of Computer Memory and Storage

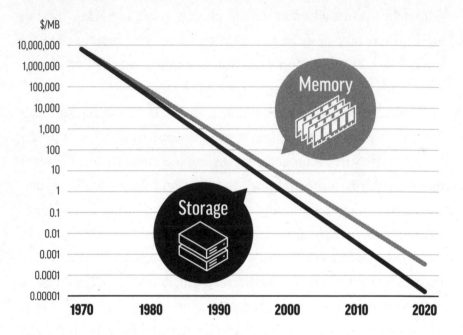

2003 to 200 mbps using 4G today and will soon become a thousand times faster as 5G takes over in the coming years.

What this means is that all of the limitations that forced music to be compressed and compromised have disappeared as technology has advanced. There is no longer any need for us to compromise.

There have been similar advancements in the sensors used in cameras and phones, yet we've not seen their manufacturers reluctant to incorporate them. They've embraced change and offer upgraded models each year focused on better quality imaging, well beyond what was originally assumed to be "good enough." Similarly, we've not seen the high-definition flat-panel television manufacturers refrain from offering us new models that provide

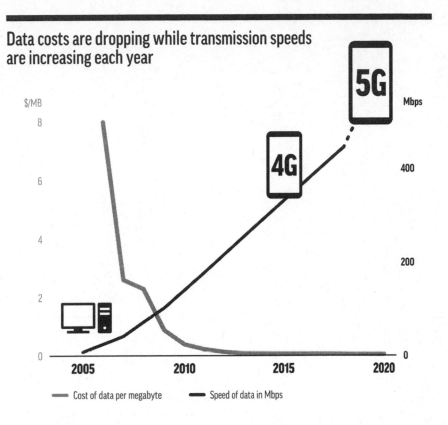

Data costs are dropping while transmission speeds are increasing each year

Cost of data per megabyte — Speed of data in Mbps

pictures with ever higher resolution and greater dynamic range. In fact, it's completely normal and expected for technology companies to make continuous and rapid improvement in all their products, driven by the advances in components, infrastructure, and manufacturing techniques.

What's so disconcerting is that we have not seen this with the audio quality of recorded music. Among all the advances in consumer digital technology, music has been the exception. Quality has actually decreased over time. We're seeing more musicians recording at lower-quality audio, and more people listening to lower-quality files, compared to what was done in the past. Clearly, something is amiss and needs to be changed.

Chapter 3 | Neil

HOW I DISCOVERED WE WERE LOSING THE MUSIC

My efforts to save music are not the result of a recent realization; it's something that's been a big concern of mine for more than thirty years. I've written about it, spoken about it, and have attempted to do something about it. Because of what's happening to music, I'm putting a huge amount of my time and energy into this, and I'll continue to do so for as long as I am able. And let me be clear about this: I'm not doing this just because of my own art. No, I'm doing it because of all the great art that's been made over the last nine or ten decades.

Until the 1980s, all music that's ever been recorded has been done using an analog format, such as tape and vinyl, capturing every detail and nuance. Unfortunately, these physical media are deteriorating over time. While many of these archival masters are being transferred, they're preserved mostly at CD quality. That's not a solution, because digital CDs are such low quality and can't match the quality of the original analog recordings. As the analog tapes continue to deteriorate, all we will have left of all our recorded music will be the lower-quality digital copies. In essence, high-quality recorded performances are vanishing from existence.

This loss of quality is the consequence of the many roadblocks that have been erected by record and technology companies, roadblocks that have prevented musicians from bringing the full experience of their art—equal to the quality that was originally recorded in the studios—to the people. These roadblocks are in turn the result of financial and pricing considerations with no regard for the music itself. Imagine if the paintings of all the great masters of art were preserved only in photographs. Sure, we would still see the images and colors, but where are the brushstrokes, the textures, and the varying thicknesses of the paint?

That's the reality of music today, and as a result we can't enjoy the art nearly as much as we used to. These roadblocks have taken away a lot of the magic of the art, its soul—reduced it, and sucked all the life out of it. Yes, we can recognize the songs and the lyrics and say that it has a good melody and is performed by a good group or individual. But there's so much more to music than just being able to recognize it. We have to be able to *feel* it. When singers sing, we feel something special. That's the whole idea of music—without it, people would just be talking.

There wouldn't be music if it weren't one of the greatest ways of communicating that humanity has ever created. And all the sound recordings of the last hundred years or so are victims. Victims of the digital technology that we now have. Digital technology is capable of preserving music at the highest quality, but instead it's being compressed to a much lower quality—nowhere close to the level at which it was originally performed—and there is no reason for that in the twenty-first century.

Look back at the history of recorded music to better understand what's happening. The first seventy years of recorded sound used analog formats, ultimately relying on very high-end tape recorders. As a result, these recordings captured every part of the performance. There were downsides, of course. The limitations of the recording media sometimes introduced background noise or a slight hissing sound. But these recordings contained *all* the sounds that were heard in the studio during the original performance; no parts were ever removed intentionally.

HERE'S THE PROBLEM

Analog media, whether tape or vinyl, has a limited life span, while digital does not. With digital, the content is not recorded as it was played; it is recorded as bits, which can be transferred around without introducing errors. This allows music producers to make multiple identical copies without limit. It's a step removed from the original, but you can have as many copies as you want. This has become the new standard. But while digital files can be preserved forever, they do not capture the original feeling and depth of the music content, especially at the lowest resolutions offered by numerous technology companies that sell downloads and streaming services.

Some digital recordings created at the highest level of digital quality available do have the potential of capturing the original

Comparison between Vinyl, CD, MP3, and Streaming

Amount of Data

VINYL
Hi-Res Analog
100%

HI-RES
Digital
90%

CD
25%

MP3
Today's Streaming
5%

performances for listening and archiving. These high-res recordings contain about 90 percent of the data captured in an analog format. As we move our culture's older recordings from analog to digital, we need to do it at this high level of digital. If we don't, the originals will be gone. We will be stuck with CD quality forever.

CD quality is greatly inferior to the best digital quality. A CD recording strips out about 75 percent of the data captured in the original analog recording, leaving us with a representation of the original that uses just a quarter of the data. MP3 streaming quality is even worse, stripping 95 percent of the original data.

Meanwhile, the analog tapes in the vaults are all disintegrating, even though they're just sitting there and not being used. These are the tapes on which thousands of artists recorded their original performances—the world's great artists, representing the entire remaining history of recorded music.

If we want to listen to these analog master tapes or make a copy of them, we would need to carefully take the tapes out of the vaults, bake the tapes to warm them up, unreel them, and carefully copy them on the first or second playback. Each day we wait it gets harder to do before the tapes will eventually just disintegrate and fall apart. This is why it's so important to make high-resolution digital copies now to prevent losing the history of music. The art of doing this correctly is alive with the archivists and mastering engineers of the biggest record companies. So why isn't the music industry making high-resolution digital copies of all these original analog recordings? They have the ability to do this. But they're not interested in the expense of doing this if it's just to preserve the content for historical reasons. The only reason they would do this is if they could sell them. To bother, they need to have a market.

TWO OBSTACLES

First, record companies have no market because they've priced these high-res recordings very high, often two or three times more than a CD or MP3 copy. No streaming company can afford to offer them, and consumers can't afford to buy them. Most people don't want to pay two or three times more than a standard download, even to get higher quality, and because no one is buying them, there are no machines to play them on, so even less high-res music is being produced.

Second, the playback devices most readily available to consumers are cell phones, designed for playback of CD or lower-quality files that are stored on or streamed to the device. There are few devices available to play high-resolution music in the convenient way people are accustomed to hearing their music. Most cell phones currently cannot play back high-resolution audio files without adding an additional piece of technology—a high-quality digital-to-analog converter (DAC). The version built into the phone, or integrated into the headphone adapter in the case of iPhones, is usually limited to CD quality or lower, so this external DAC would bypass it. This component, which costs only a few dollars, would then allow the phone to play high-resolution music. The problem, of course, is the bulkiness and lack of convenience. Most people want a single portable device, not a multipart, some-assembly-required player. And because people no longer experience high-res music, they don't know what they're missing. Fewer and fewer people will ever experience the true magic and soul of the greatest recordings ever made.

THE HISTORY

The degradation of music began with the premium pricing of high-res audio by the record companies. Over the past few decades, record companies segmented their products by creating a multitude of versions of the very same performance, each at different levels of quality. They charge more money as the quality goes higher and higher, consequently making music itself more elitist, as the best quality is reserved for those at the top.

In addition, customers have had to purchase the same album time after time as formats changed. First on vinyl, then cassette tape, then CD, and now at several levels of digital. These are issues that have happened relatively recently compared to the life span of recorded music. Rightfully, music fans have lost patience with record companies and don't want to keep buying the same performance time and time again.

But it's now the twenty-first century, and it's become possible to have *one* format that plays all recorded music at its highest level as well as every level lower than the highest, when needed. I, along with others, have proven that, and we will tell you more in the coming pages.

CDs

In the eighties when CDs were first introduced, everybody was talking about how great the sound quality was. There was no buzzing, no clicking, no hissing or popping. But many of us soon discovered that CDs had their own issues, just different ones from what came before. They *would* click and pop and would repeat and repeat. As I spent more time listening to CD recordings, I also listened for overtones, air, echo, and nuances in the music, but found them to be almost gone. Just the surface of the music was there. No depth remained. That is where the soul of music used to live.

As I experienced CDs in the first year that they were available, I began to understand their limitations more and more. My awareness came from years of making music and spending many days and hours creating final recordings using a process called mixing. When I did the mixing of my recordings, I would create the mix from analog tapes. I did this for years and years, so I understood what the music feels like and what's involved in the mixing process.

WHAT MIXING IS

Mixing involves balancing different tracks that have been recorded on a multitrack recorder and transferring them to a two-track recorder to create a stereo mix or a mono recording. We might start with anywhere from eight to thirty-two tracks. We would sometimes have six mics on one track. Sounds and vocals are divided up into tracks, so they can be blended; instruments can also be blended to create the final work, the balanced master blend of all the tracks. In the end, the sound would usually turn out great.

Mixing is rewarding work. It involves changing volumes, shifting equalization, adding echo, taking echo away, placing it to the left, placing to the right, to the center, center left, center right, panning it back and forth while recording so it moves. It might involve putting delays on the echo, so it shows up late, which gives it more of a huge sound. (Phil Spector used to do that with Jack Nitzsche. In the sixties, he developed the Wall of Sound, a production technique where everybody's playing their instruments at once and the sound is recorded in an echo chamber. What you get is the microphone picking up all these reverberated sounds—all those things are what goes into a mix.)

So, if you take most of that away with CDs—the echoes, the sense of spaciousness, and the nuances of each track—you can feel what is missing. But you have to have heard the real thing to miss it.

TWO ERAS OF RECORDED SOUND

Before the 1980s, multitrack tape machines were analog, varying from eight to thirty-two tracks, mixed to another analog tape recorder, stereo, or earlier, mono. That was how we made our master recordings.

The first thing that happened in the digital era is that we started mixing to two-track stereo digital at the recording sessions for CDs. Everything got sampled at 44.1 kHz with 16-bit accuracy in the machines at that time. In the eighties, the Sony multitrack and two-track digital recording machines defined what became the standard for CDs. People would say that it was just as good as analog, that you couldn't hear the difference, that no one could tell the difference, that any difference was inaudible. It was all marketing and had nothing to do with reality. Yet we were backed into this level of quality by what the machines were capable of at that time.

Some listeners were fooled. Even some of my musician friends thought that digital was better. There is a great producer, Mutt Lange, who felt that digital was better because the signal-to-noise difference was greater with digital; there was no hiss and the signal could be really loud and separated from the background noise. If you wanted to get a big drum sound and put a lot of echo on it, and then have it go away quickly, you could get it really loud and have it quickly stop using digital. And that was something he thought was great about digital.

I agree that this characteristic of a high signal-to-noise ratio can be much better with digital, but all the other things about digital were not great. The tonal quality, the granularity of the sound, the details all were missing. In other words, just because the technology was new didn't mean it was better.

Here's an important consideration between analog and digital:

With analog it's a reflection of the original, with digital it's a reconstituted version of the original.

I always like to use an example of Shasta Lake on a completely calm day with no breeze. The lake is like a mirror, so if you look into it, you can see Mount Shasta upside down in the water. All the beauty of Mount Shasta is right there in the reflection, and anybody can easily reverse the image in their mind to get it right side up. That's what analog is. That doesn't happen with digital.

Here's another thought:

Imagine looking through a screened window from ten feet back. Observe. Now move right up to the screen and imagine that each square in that screen is averaged to just one color, the most dominant color that you can see through that square. Now step back, imagining that every square is limited to just its one dominant color. Look.

The amount of squares in the screen is the resolution. The larger the square, the lower the resolution.

High resolution = fine screen

Low resolution = chicken wire

With digital music, the original reflection really is not there. There's no universe of sound, there's no mirror in the lake. It's a bunch of averaged squares, and because it's not the same thing, your sensitive body isn't reacting the same way to a bunch of squares. The body is going, "I hear it and I recognize it, but I just don't feel it. I don't feel it like I used to feel it. What's happening? Am I going deaf? Am I getting old? Do I not experience this anymore? Did I wear myself out? What's happening?"

Maybe you went to war and fired a gun for ten years. Maybe you were captain of a battleship. Whatever the hell you did, maybe your hearing is severely degraded. I can tell you from my own experience that no matter how much you hurt your ears, it doesn't affect the *quality* of what you are still hearing. You only hear what you can. When you listen to analog, the magic is still there. You pick up the real shit. You may not hear as much of the high end, not as much of this frequency or that frequency. But what you hear is the real thing.

Is there some level of digital that's equivalent to analog? I don't know, I don't think so. You can fool the body or the mind, but you can't fool the soul. You can understand what it is. You may react, "Wow, this sounds great." When I listen to Pono high res at 192/24 or my Xstream by NYA high-res streaming at full resolution through great speakers, I know the audio sounds great. Does it *feel* as good as what it's a copy of? I don't think it does. No, I don't think so.

ANALOG CASSETTES

Cassette tapes, which were popular in the late seventies and early eighties, provided a good solution in their time and allowed for music mobility. But the cassettes had more hiss than the originals. They didn't have the same big huge sound as a record or a tape master. When you listened to a cassette on a good high-fidelity system, the tape would start playing with a noisy background sound, something like *shshshshshshsh*, before the music would begin. That was because the tape was moving so slowly, and the background noise prevailed. It was the limitation of the technology at that time. Nonetheless, when the music started playing, if it was loud enough and the signal-to-noise (*shshshshshshsh*) ratio was great enough, you still heard a lot of the music that was a reflection of a reflection of a reflection of the original. That was how many generations the music had to go to get from the original recording to the cassette.

And yet, the cassette tape was a whole other world of quality from something like an MP3, which was not only not the original master, or a reflection of the original master, but maybe an eight-times degraded version of a digital reconstitution. It was, and is, the ugly sound sold to mass consumers today.

THE CLEAR DIFFERENCE

So, yes, there's a clear difference between digital and analog. With that said, there can still be great digital, though never as great as the original analog. Great digital would have to struggle to be as good as an average analog recording—and still never make it. High-resolution digital might sound better, and it might sound more precise, and it might even sound crystal clear, and your reaction might be, "Wow, this is great!" But when you sit down and listen repeatedly, listen to the analog and then listen to the digital—listen to the music, not analyzing it in your mind, but letting your soul listen to it—you'll gravitate toward the analog. The analog is always more satisfying because it feeds the body more of a universe of sound. It feeds your soul. That is the magic of music.

Different parts of your body react differently to the music. Your mind reacts one way and your soul reacts another way. Here's an example.

I've been listening to *Reactor*, a record I made in the eighties. We've been listening to CDs of it for a long time. Then I remastered it to a 192-digital version for high-res streaming and we went back and listened to our analog master. *Wow, that sounded great!* In the process we made a high-resolution digital 192/24 master from the original analog. It's the best digital ever. It sounds fantastic and it's convenient—but it's not the original.

When we made the analog stereo tapes, we made the sound as good as it could be, mixing from the original multitrack tape. I immediately mixed to two analog tracks for a stereo master because the analog starts deteriorating right away. The first playback is a wonderful sound, but the tape degrades each time it passes over the heads of the machine. If the tape machine is not aligned perfectly, it might wipe off some of the sound, so that it actually breaks down faster. From experience, I know that if I'm remixing the next day and my tape machine is not perfect, after three or four playbacks, I'll go, *Wow, let's compare this to the first rough we made last night.* I'll discover that what we did today doesn't have something we heard last night. The rough mix sounds a lot better than the polished one we just completed. It's not because of the work we've done with it; it's because of how many times we've run the tape over the heads. I have used many original "rough" mixes because I could not get the magic back when I remixed at a later time. My rough mixes captured the sound of the multitrack the first time it was played.

I have recorded analog and then gone direct to digital from the analog. I've also recorded direct to digital and I've compared the results from each. I always find the analog is going to sound better over the long run, as with the example of *Reactor* when we created a vinyl record of it. It's like night and day, better than 192. It's amazingly great. You get lost in it. You're listening to it. It feeds your body. It's the real thing. It's like drinking water from a natural spring instead of water from a reservoir that's been conditioned. It hasn't been screwed with. That's the difference.

So that's why I'm so passionate about preserving what has already been recorded at the highest level. I can hear the difference. I can feel the difference. I know what I hear, and I know what I feel, and I want to preserve that for eternity, so it's not lost in the future. Because once it's lost, others will not be able to experience what I can experience now.

THE DIGITAL AGE

We're stuck in the digital age. So, we must copy our original analog recordings now before those analog masters disappear. In another few decades we won't have the ability to copy them. By the time people realize what they're missing, it may be too late for them to get it back. And record companies continue selling crap while pricing high res out of the market.

How do the record companies react to my pleas? They don't react much at all, yet. The heads of the companies I have spoken with agree with me, but what can they do? The world wants and is satisfied with the low-price, low-quality material. I've implored music executives to ask their financial people how much money they've actually made by charging so much for their high-resolution content. What has the company actually made from it? They're the ones trying to make the companies profitable and successful by placing a value on the music. So, they have chosen to place a high price on the high-quality version and a moderate price on their mediocre quality and a low price on their bad quality.

People are buying the bad quality because it's cheap and convenient. Few are willing to spend more to buy the high quality. Record companies get little profit from selling high-quality content. This has terrible consequences that go well beyond the recording industry.

With no sales and little availability of high-quality content, most hardware products, especially smartphones, are being designed to only play bad-quality content. With record companies charging two to three times more for high res, they can't sell it, there's no market for it, and there's little interest in others accommodating it in their hardware products.

Meanwhile, more time goes by as the analog masters sit in the vaults and degrade each day, becoming susceptible to catastrophic events that could destroy them. Perhaps from a fire or a failure of an air conditioner in their temperature-controlled vaults. These tapes are almost like living things; they have limited lives and they age. If we don't take care of them, they will die. They're like flowers that need water to keep them alive.

It's understandable that record companies are focused on profits. It's not that they don't want the heritage of music to continue to exist. They love music, too. They just don't realize that their bean counters are screwing them. That they are charging too much while they *should* charge basically the same amount for everything and save the music that made record companies successful in the first place.

That's what I'm doing on my NYA website. I charge $1.29 for a digital master and it doesn't matter what the resolution is. It can be an MP3, or it can be a 192. They are all the same price. I've been able to negotiate this singular price, regardless of resolution, because of my relationship with my record company. They are only giving me this deal because they believe in my premise and because I've earned it. I've been working with them for fifty years and they are letting me do whatever I want.

IMPROVING STREAMING

Jay-Z has done a lot with Tidal to improve streaming quality. I don't agree with their technology, but I think they are trying to do something good. I find the technology they bought into, Master Quality Authenticated (MQA), limiting. While there are people who think that's something innovative or important, I'm not in that camp. I believe you leave the music alone. You use the original bits and you play them back. And that's it. That's all you need. You can't improve music by adding something in between it and the listener.

MQA is just another format, another manipulation of the original performance, and proprietary, as well. It is obsolete—we're past the time it was designed for. We're trying to get away from formats. All formats. There is only a need for one method that plays all masters at native quality or as close to it as the streaming bit rate will allow: high-res digital.

GOING FORWARD

There's no denying that we are in the digital age and that music will always be digital going forward. There's nothing we can do about that. We've moved away from the analog age. That's only in the past.

If we want to preserve what we have, however, we'd better copy it, and we'd better do it at the highest level of digital so that we have saved it as best we could while it's still available. Because it is going away—even as we talk about it, more of it disintegrates. That's the crux of why I am doing this. To save music for eternity. To save the art of recorded sound. To feel the music.

Chapter 9 | Phil

NEIL WAS NOT ALONE

*N*eil was not alone in his concern about the degradation of audio quality. Craig Kallman experienced a similar revelation in the early eighties when he was a teenager living with his family in New York City. He was an avid music fan who began collecting vinyl records when he was just twelve. He worked as a DJ after high school and on weekends at some of the city's most famous nightclubs, including the Palladium and Danceteria. By then Craig had become a big vinyl collector and was using his DJ earnings to purchase records along with the audio equipment to play them. That was when he learned about the major labels' invention that was supposedly going to revolutionize the music industry with its superior sound using digital technology.

Craig was intrigued and excited, and couldn't wait to listen to this new high-tech thing called the compact disc. Once CDs went on sale, he began buying an assortment along with the best CD player available. He rigged up two turntables alongside his new CD player and hooked them up to his mixer so that he could, at the flick of a switch, go back and forth between the vinyl and the compact disc, to see just how much better it was. He bought CDs of Neil Young's *Harvest*, Led Zeppelin, Sly and the Family Stone, Fleetwood Mac, Hot Tuna, and Taj Mahal, plus some other favorites, and played them all, switching between both formats, listening intently and taking notes.

As always, he found that the vinyl recordings were warm, musical, and highly euphonic, giving him goose bumps and chills. But, to his amazement, when he switched to the compact disc versions of the exact same recordings, he didn't feel anything from the CDs. They were cold and brittle sounding.

He was shocked by what he heard. Kallman was terrified that the music industry had declared that the CD was going to be the future of the music business, when it was so much worse than what it was replacing.

That was when he accelerated his vinyl acquisition and embarked on a mission he's still on today. Because he didn't want to discover new music on a CD and not be able to listen to it at its highest possible quality, he decided he must own all the world's music on vinyl. This way he'd have in his collection all of the music in its most emotionally impactful form, the vinyl disc. To Kallman, vinyl was, by far, the medium that elicited the most visceral, biological, emotional response; the most potent, powerful response. CDs were a poor substitute, making vinyl even more important.

Kallman began chronicling the entire history of recorded music by visiting libraries and bookstores, buying every book on the subject, and researching every important artist in every genre of music, with the intent of acquiring the entire discography of these artists on vinyl. At the time, for example, Neil Young had thirty-seven albums. Kallman compiled a list and bought each one of them. He did this for every important or notable artist in every genre: rock, jazz, soul, blues, folk, disco, reggae, world, electronic, soundtracks, *everything*—and bought them all.

Kallman's vinyl collection now numbers 1.1 million albums, one of the largest private collections in the world, motivated by his love of music and wanting to preserve the true sound of the original performances.

After Kallman graduated from Brown University, he started his own record company, Big Beat Records, selling records door to door to mom-and-pop record stores up and down the streets of Manhattan. His business grew from a one-man company with revenues of $50,000 in its first year to $2 million three years later. In 1991 his company was acquired by Warner Music Group, and Kallman is now the chairman and CEO of Warner's Atlantic Records.

In the early nineties, after Big Beat's acquisition and from his new role at Warner, Kallman became a lone crusader for high-quality sound

Craig Kallman and Neil Young
(*Photo by Vince Bucci*)

in an industry that was prioritizing profits, convenience, and durability at the expense of true optimum sound. He has always thought that by killing vinyl and replacing it with CDs, the music industry had done a major disservice to real music lovers.

Chapter 5 | Neil

THE BIRTH OF PONO

Based on what I was hearing in the studio, and then what I heard on the CDs, I kept thinking, *Man, we are really going in the wrong direction.* And then when I listened to MP3 recordings on my phone, it was so much worse than the CD. Then came streaming, and it was the worst quality ever. We kept degrading music over and over again.

At the time, I assumed that streaming would never be able to get to the level of high res, so even though we considered it, we went in the direction of high-quality downloads and a great music player. In retrospect, I was wrong, but it would be a few more years before the technology emerged to make high-res streaming viable. In the meantime, I knew I just had to do something!

MY FIRST SOLUTION

I decided it was time to offer a solution—a music player and a download store so listeners could enjoy the highest-quality audio possible. My vision was a system that created a convenient way for music lovers to find, purchase, and listen to the finest recordings ever made with no compromise and no degradation. It was time to do something.

I went to Warner Music Group, my longtime record company, and told them I wanted to build a music player and start a download service for high-resolution music. They knew how I felt about audio quality because I've complained to them for years about what was happening in the industry. I asked to be allowed to resell their music, much in the way that Apple, Amazon, and Google were doing, but I wanted to focus on high-res content. Record companies already had licensing agreements to allow these tech companies to sell their music and pay them a percentage of their sales, and my goal was to do much the same.

The then-head of Warner Music, Lyor Cohen, introduced me to Craig Kallman. Lyor told me that Craig would be a good person to work with on this because Craig had also voiced his concerns about music quality, and he had been a strong advocate for better audio quality within Warner.

I really like Craig; he's a really cool guy. He understands recording quality and he has been a crusader for this cause ever since he entered the music business. We hit it off well with similar sentiments about how people deserve to experience music.

BOB STUART

Craig, along with Mike Jbara, another Warner executive, introduced me to Bob Stuart, one of the founders of Meridian, a
high-end hardware audio equipment company in Cambridge,
England. They loved Stuart and I think had invested some money
in his company. They thought that Stuart had some good ideas for
improving music quality and, with that mutual interest, we might
find a way to all work together.

Stuart's contribution would be to provide some new technology he had been working on for many years that was designed to
reduce the size of the high-res music files without reducing the
audio quality. The high cost of memory in the 1980s was a big factor in the design of music players, and this led to the need for the
compression of music to reduce the amount of memory it used,
which unfortunately meant much poorer quality.

APPLE

The first iPod music player was introduced in late 2001 and
was made possible by the miniature hard disc drive invented by
Toshiba, a 5-gigabyte drive that was less than two inches in diam-
eter. Apple decided that they wanted their new product to hold an
entire music collection—thousands of albums—which required
them to use a file format that compressed the music files to about
one-twentieth the normal size.

That idea of having a large quantity of songs in your pocket, along with the reality of expensive memory, led to a decision that continues to have a profound effect on music quality today. Apple squeezed music files to fit the technology they had, even though it degraded the music greatly. These were called MP3 files, a format developed in 1993 and made popular by file-sharing sites.

STUART'S SOLUTION

Stuart told me that Meridian had been trying to address the loss of quality of these compressed MP3 files by creating a better way to reduce file sizes. I often said to him that it's less of a problem now, as memory prices have come down and would continue to decline, but he had been working on it for so long, I think he came to believe it was more important than it really was. Still, with this feature, my music player would have a unique way to distinguish itself—high res requiring less memory. And besides, he had the support of my record company, whose help I needed.

We met with Stuart in New York and got our attorneys together to create the beginnings of a deal to work with each other. Stuart was always somewhat vague about exactly what he was doing, but I thought it would make my downloaded music more efficient, particularly when we would play it on a phone or portable device.

GETTING PONO GOING

I brought in a few people to help me get off the ground, including a local entrepreneur, Mark Goldstein; a software engineer, Jason Rubenstein; and Mike Nuttall, a really great industrial designer.

We talked about developing both a player and a download music service where we'd sell the content for the player. We wanted to do it all. We had big eyes and strong ambitions.

We would have these meetings at my ranch in Northern California, and Stuart would fly over from England with his engineer and talk a lot about how he could help us. But, as time went on, we still had no formal arrangement; it was always unclear where we were on the deal and who was doing what.

I kept asking my manager, the late Elliot Roberts, "Do we have a contract? Is Stuart joining us?" But still, no contract. Finally, I said we couldn't keep going on this way. We needed to make progress and not just keep talking. We needed to move forward and develop a music store and a player focused on high res.

We went ahead and formed a company. Warner put in five hundred thousand dollars, and I put in about half of that, and we each owned half of the company. This allowed us to finally begin. I named the company "Pono Music." Pono, which means "the one" and "righteousness" in Hawaiian, is a word I like a lot, and embodies the spirit of what we were all about.

We had lots of discussions about the hardware. Display or no display, a stand-alone device or something that connected to a phone. This was around the time when iPhones were starting to sell in big quantities and even beginning to replace the iPod music players. There was a lot of appeal in trying to leverage off the iPhone, because it already had many of the things we needed: a big, clear touch display; an operating system; and a user interface. It was essentially a pocket computer.

But iPhones didn't have good enough electronics to play back the digital music files, and most phones today still don't. I'm referring to the electronics used to convert the digital music files to analog, which is required to drive headphones and speakers, the devices we use to bring music to our ears. The electronics are made up of two sections: a DAC (digital to analog converter) circuit and an amplifier part that increases the level of the analog signals sent to the headphones or speakers.

Concepts showing design evolution
(*Courtesy of Mike Nuttall*)

One idea we had was to build some kind of a flat box that would attach to an iPhone. The box would have a much better DAC and amplifier electronics and lots of memory to store the large music files. We'd also need to develop an app that could be used to manage, select, and play back the music.

I liked the idea a lot, because it meant carrying just one device and reducing the work we would need to do. But there was a big concern about whether we'd get the cooperation of Apple for this add-on product. Apple required their approval of any device that connects to the phone using their special port on the bottom. We were proposing adding a better music player compared to their built-in music app—probably not something they'd be very happy about.

Apple's rule for approving add-ons was to not make a decision until you gave them a finished product to test—a big problem for us. In addition, an add-on device would also need to work with different models of iPhones and Android phones, so it could not just be one product.

I had met with Steve Jobs in the past, and I knew how Apple would feel. While he appreciated high-res music and listened to vinyl himself, he had no interest in high res for his products, and this belief was one of the reasons that our music was deteriorating. When we spoke together, he told me his customers were perfectly satisfied with MP3 quality. He had one standard for himself and another for his customers. As he said, "We are a consumer company."

ANOTHER IDEA—THE PONO PLAYER

Because of these potential difficulties of working with Apple, and with the need to make additional products for Android phones, I started to prefer the idea of a separate music player, because it could be used anywhere: in the car, at home, or on an airplane. I wanted it to be something people would carry with them to listen to music anytime and anywhere. That was what we finally decided to do. We wouldn't need to worry about designing around the iPhone and be at Apple's mercy with a product that attached. We decided to do a stand-alone player.

I just wanted an easy way to listen to music that sounded great. While there were a few other players available, they were either pretty bad or ridiculously expensive, some costing way more than a thousand dollars. The good ones were focused on elite customers because only they could afford them. That was all wrong. High-res music should not be just for elites—it should be for everyone.

We also needed a music store that sold high-res music. There were some other music stores; the best one that I knew about was HDtracks. But, like a lot of technology for the audiophile, it was complicated to use and not meant for the average listener. To buy an album, you'd have to choose from a lot of different formats with strange abbreviations that even I didn't always understand. And you couldn't buy singles from their high-res albums. I wanted our store just to sell the best resolution available for any album and nothing else.

So, as we went through our options, this was what we finally decided Pono would be: an affordable music player that sounded like God and an easy way to buy the content at the highest resolution available. Perhaps I was naïve in thinking we'd be successful where others hadn't, but I felt no one else had looked at it this way and that we would offer some real benefits to those who just wanted to find and listen to great quality music.

For Pono to be successful, I needed agreements with the major record companies—Warner Music Group, Sony Music, and Universal Music Group—to get permission to sell music in our store. Getting investments was dependent on these deals. A deal with only one record company would not be enough.

ELLIOT ROBERTS

Most of the other tech companies that built their own music stores, like Apple and Amazon, had to put up millions of dollars for those rights. Fortunately, I was able to get the three major record companies to do it without paying those huge fees, based on my relationships, reputation, and being well known in the industry. It took a lot of work, a lot of negotiations, and the help of expensive lawyers to put these agreements in place. Most of all, it was the hard work of my manager, Elliot Roberts, that got this done.

That was a major milestone, and I was appreciative of the record companies' support that made Pono possible. But I was also working to help them, whether they realized it or not, by trying to bring better music to the world.

Looking back, I probably got blindsided by Warner when they wanted 50 percent of Pono, but I suppose it's kind of normal. A year later, they didn't pick up their option and they lost their shares, which blew their minds. Lyor Cohen, Warner CEO and now global head of music for YouTube, called and was so surprised about it, but Elliot said, "You're done. You guys didn't pick up your option. You owned half of the company and now you don't." They were pissed, but we realized they were no longer doing anything to help Pono.

I next began looking for some advisors. I had never run a company like this and needed help. I brought in Gigi Brisson, a neighbor of mine in Hawaii who ran a small investment company. My friend Marc Benioff, CEO of Salesforce, introduced me to Rick Cohen, a corporate lawyer who worked for him and Gigi. Elliot Roberts, my manager and friend of nearly fifty years at the time, played a huge role at Pono. He knew the industry like no one else and he would turn out to be invaluable to keeping us going as long as we did. Elliot filled the role of COO, while I started out as CEO.

For the next six months, progress was slow, and we were spending lots of money. I never realized product development and lawyers could both be so expensive. The development of the player seemed to go very slowly, and I was getting impatient. I'd be given presentations with various options, asking me to make choices about things that I had little idea about. Although we had a lot of smart people, we had no real leader for the product development. Finally, after nearly a year, I was told we were almost out of money. We had spent a lot, but we were far from seeing any semblance of a product. I knew what I wanted, but getting there was very frustrating.

I discussed this with Elliot and Craig, and we decided we needed to move in another direction. I wanted my own team, and a stronger one to develop the player. Craig told me he had met someone who might be able to help—Phil Baker. I asked Craig to give him a call.

Chapter 6 | Phil

MEETING NEIL

*I*t all began with a phone call one weekend. On Saturday, February 11, 2012, I received a call from Craig Kallman. He said he was with Neil Young, who wanted to speak with me. I had met Craig, the CEO of Atlantic Records, a few weeks earlier at the Consumer Electronics Show (CES) in Las Vegas. He was introduced to me by my friend Larry Reich, who explained that Craig might need some design help for a project he was working on. We met and had a short conversation; I gave him a copy of the book I had written about product design, *From Concept to Consumer*, and he said he'd get back to me.

Neil picked up the phone and explained to me that he was trying to develop a music player, but was frustrated by the slow progress being made, and wondered if I could be of help. He explained how important his effort was—that it was literally to save the quality of audio. It seemed quite interesting to me. Of course, anything would seem interesting when it might involve working with Neil Young.

Little did I know that this phone call would lead to a multi-year adventure that I could hardly have imagined, one that took me from the discipline I knew well, product development, to new areas that included the music and entertainment industries, and to a wonderful friendship with Neil. As someone who was a part of the consumer tech industry for much of my career, it also provided me with an entirely new perspective on the harm technology was causing music.

The following Thursday, I flew to San Francisco to meet with Neil and his team to hear more about the project. Over the previous few days I'd read up on digital audio design to refresh my memory, including all of the technical terms, such as sampling rates, bit depths, DAC, FLAC, and the like.

It wasn't that I was unfamiliar with audio. I used to be a big audio hobbyist and had owned wonderful high-fidelity equipment, which I had purchased when I lived in Massachusetts. At the time, I was a product design engineer at Polaroid Corporation in Cambridge, a short walk from some of the iconic audio companies, such as KLH and Acoustic Research, that I'd visit whenever they announced a new product. I was a huge fan of my AR-3a speakers, my Fisher receiver, Dual turntable, Nakamichi tape deck, and KLH radios and all-in-one music systems. I also had a sizable collection of vinyls that I pampered.

One of my most memorable purchases was the original Sony Walkman, a simple blue metallic cassette player that I'd take, along with a stack of tapes, on my many trips to Asia while traveling for Polaroid. Years later, I bought the first iPod, because it was one of those breakthrough gadgets promising so much, but it was a big disappointment, and I couldn't tolerate the poor audio quality. That seemed about the time that I began losing interest in audio equipment, probably because the music quality had lost its appeal. I had never thought much about why my interest waned, but now I realize I've not used my current stereo system, including the four floor-standing speakers that have been sitting idle in my living room, for years.

I was unsure what to expect at the meeting but was looking forward to it, heightened by the opportunity to possibly work with a famous artist that I had enjoyed listening to for years. I had seen Neil several times in live performances at his Bridge School concerts, a yearly event he used to run in Mountain View, California. I remember one of those concerts where he brought Simon and Garfunkel to the stage for one of their rare reunions.

Prior to meeting with Neil, my son, Dan—a chef and restaurant owner with his wife, Holly, in Marin County, north of San Francisco—gave me some suggestions based on his experience in hosting celebrities at his restaurant. In a very serious tone, he said, "When you meet Neil, act naturally, just as you would do as if you were meeting an ordinary person. Don't be fawning or gushing and just be yourself. That's what celebrities want. And, whatever you do, don't take a picture or ask him for his autograph!"

I flew from my home in San Diego to SFO, picked up a rental car, and drove toward Neil's ranch, ending up on a two-lane highway that straddles the ridges of the Santa Cruz Mountains, forming the western boundary of Silicon Valley. It was about a forty-minute ride. As instructed, I parked my car in the lot of a local landmark, Alice's Restaurant. The lot was populated by numerous motorcycles and a few cars and trucks. I looked around and saw a large Cadillac SUV with the driver motioning to me. I jumped into the back seat, and we were off.

The SUV drove a short bit, then turned onto a narrow road surrounded by redwood trees and heavy brush. We drove more than six miles along winding, half-paved roads, through alternating woods and open fields, stopping on occasion to allow an oncoming car to pass. We went through two electric gates, passing a couple of other houses on large plots of land, and finally into a wide clearing with an open pasture that was the beginning of Neil's Broken Arrow Ranch. We had to stop once to allow the alpacas and cows to move off the road before we crossed a wooden bridge through a grove of trees and approached a structure on the right that was Neil's office. The one-story log-cabin building had an old-fashioned gas pump in front, along with an old Cadillac parked on the side, one of the many classics in Neil's car collection. There was an old railroad caboose in back, used for another office, and a large barn next door that I later learned had a huge electric train layout. I was greeted by Neil with a friendly handshake and by Elliot Roberts, Neil's manager, an icon himself with an illustrious career managing many famous artists, including Joni Mitchell, Bob Dylan, and Tom Petty.

The building was one large open room with a wood-burning stove, a desk in the corner, a conference table in the front, and three of Neil's restored automobiles at the rear. We exchanged amenities, I gave Neil a copy of my book, and, once Craig Kallman joined us, we sat down to discuss Neil's efforts to create the product he wanted to build.

Neil explained how frustrated he was that music quality had deteriorated, even as technology advanced. Music was being compressed just for convenience and cost. He explained how he had been vocal about this whenever he got the opportunity and was intent on offering a solution, so others could experience how much better audio quality could be.

Neil brought me up to date on how long he had been working on this and how he needed my help to accelerate the design and development of his music player. He explained how he, along with his label, Warner Music, had spent almost a million dollars in this effort and were frustrated that they had little to show for it, mostly PowerPoint presentations. They had been using a large Silicon Valley design consultancy but had made little progress.

I wasn't all that surprised. I've been developing products for companies for years and have learned that the Valley is filled with large design firms that promise much more than they deliver, yet still manage to collect their large fees, often taking advantage of inexperienced clients. They can take twice as long as needed, resulting in twice the cost, under the guise of being extra thorough, but with little regard for the client's limited budget. While there are many Silicon Valley design companies that do great work, without close management, projects can quickly escalate in cost.

I thought I'd be able to help Neil by taking on the development of the project as I've done many times before, using a small team of experienced specialists. But I knew I'd need to brush up on my audio expertise. I had some experience developing audio products such as headphones, earbuds, and speakers, but certainly not at the level this required. A product good enough to impact the industry? That was quite a goal and a big challenge.

My expertise is managing the design of consumer hardware products, which includes creating, assembling, and leading a team from the early concept stage, through the intricacies of engineering design, and into high-volume manufacturing. I felt very comfortable doing what I had done dozens of times before. The key was finding the right team members. I knew that if I could find strong, experienced engineers in several specific disciplines, I could help. This was a unique opportunity to make a difference with a product that meant so much to Neil.

He explained to me how important it was to provide music lovers access to the same quality of content that he hears when he's in the studio recording. Vinyl records had been faithful reproductions of the music he recorded there, but as vinyl "progressed" to the digital CD, the amount of audio information and sound quality suffered. With their iPod, Apple opted for convenience over quality and the sound further deteriorated. In fact, Neil explained that many young people have never experienced quality audio, and he was determined to change that.

We discussed how we might proceed with the development of a music player that could reproduce the high-definition sound, and I explained the approach I would take. We would need a small team of engineers to work on the industrial design, audio and other electronics, firmware, and mechanical design. And we'd need a software engineer to create the user interface.

I had a couple of people in mind, and if they were available, I expressed confidence that we could create the product much more quickly and for less cost than the approach he had been using. I agreed to get back to Neil, Elliot, and Craig with a proposal within the next few days.

As I departed, Neil thanked me for coming, gave me a hug, and seemed excited about our working together. One last thing, he asked. Would I autograph my book that I had given him?

Chapter 7 | Phil

GETTING STARTED

A revolution in product development has occurred in recent years as the result of the globalization of technology. Almost anyone with an idea can now act on it and find the needed resources to turn it into a product, particularly with help from efficient and experienced manufacturers. It used to be that only the large companies had access to the Asian factories, but now almost anyone can use these resources. China has revolutionized the process with its entrepreneurial mind-set, can-do attitude, manufacturing expertise, and huge industrial centers that build products for much of the world.

Some regions of China specialize in the manufacturing of small consumer electronics, others in computers, phones, audio, major appliances, power tools, and even paintings. Within each area are all the suppliers that provide support with components and expertise. That also means that even small product companies can take advantage of economies of scale to produce products at very low costs, often using the same manufacturers as their competitors.

This infrastructure enables small companies like Pono to be much more effective than if they had to fend for themselves. Instead they can focus on and invest in the product definition, design, engineering, sales, and marketing and rely on companies in China for manufacturing. This phenomenon of low-cost, efficient Chinese manufacturing has been responsible for the success of thousands of hardware startup companies that employ millions around the world. It's an alliance that has worked well. In fact, China's manufacturing efficiencies have resulted in more high-paying jobs in this country for those in the creative, engineering, and marketing areas, because they can rely on China to set up assembly lines, train a workforce, and manage the complex logistics of building products.[5]

PRODUCT DEVELOPMENT STEPS

Product development involves several phases, from crafting a concept all the way to manufacturing. You define clearly what you want, then design, prototype, test, and refine it until it meets all of your requirements, including fulfilling a market need—always a challenge, because that needs to be done a year or two in advance of sales.

5   James Fallows, "China Makes, The World Takes," *The Atlantic*, July/August 2007, https://www.theatlantic.com/magazine/archive/2007/07/china-makes-the-world -takes/305987/.

A LOT OF MONEY

The other requirement for developing a product is having the financial resources to fund it. And with hardware you need a lot of money, not only for the development but for building prototypes and tooling and buying parts well in advance of production and months before being paid by customers. Funding has been made a little easier with crowdsourcing platforms, where contributions are solicited from the public to support the effort. It's often a much simpler option than trying to convince investors to put money into your company.

But with crowdfunding you need to be able to provide a definitive cost and schedule much sooner than normal to get the support for your campaign—many months before you really know. As a result, most projects underestimate the cost and overpromise the delivery date.

EXCITEMENT

Still, developing products can be very exciting. It's much like embarking on a long trip with just a rough sketch of the route but few details along the way. There are invariably surprises and unexpected issues that come up. You sometimes take the wrong turn, and other times hit a dead end. But if you keep your eye on the destination, it can be a lot of fun.

With most products, you're managing several parallel development activities: mechanical, electrical, and software, each independent yet interlocking. All must come together in the end and work seamlessly with each other. And, more times than not, you don't know all of the problems that will arise until after you have actually shipped the product to hundreds or thousands of customers!

The personal reward comes from transforming an idea into a product that millions will buy and use. I had gone through this process for more than a hundred products, and while some had problems that seemed like they'd never be solved, almost every one was. Where there was a failure of a product, it was most often in attracting customers, rarely with its design or the ability to be made.

Neil's product would be the culmination of all I had done up to that time. I was confident because I had done this so many times before, had made many mistakes along the way, and had learned from them. But this product was one that could not have any mistakes because of its high visibility and importance to Neil's reputation. We'd have one chance to get it right.

Chapter 8 | Phil

BEGINNING DEVELOPMENT

*L*ess than a month after the initial meeting, I was back at the ranch for a second meeting with the team that I had begun to assemble to develop what would become the Pono music player.

Neil, Elliot, and Craig had accepted my proposal to manage the entire effort. One of the benefits of working in Silicon Valley is that it's home to some of the best experts in almost any technology field you can imagine. Because so many of us have worked at numerous companies, networking is amazingly effective; the more jobs you have, the more experts you encounter, and if you don't know the expert you need, one of your other contacts usually does. I had in mind several people based on prior experience and reputation. As a result, I was able to assemble a small team in about ten days. Never had I gotten such a positive response from those I called; they all welcomed the opportunity to work with Neil on his important pursuit. No one needed any persuasion.

THE TEAM

Mike Nuttall, a cofounder of the product design company IDEO and now out on his own, was responsible for the industrial design. I had worked with him when I first moved to Silicon Valley nearly three decades earlier; coincidentally, he had already been working with Neil and his first team. I had high regard for his capabilities and design talents. His role would be to further define the product's appearance: the controls and the interface, essentially everything that affected user interaction. He had already come up with the general shape of the player, but there was much more work to do to design all the details, including its construction, display, color, finish, materials, user interface, and controls.

I brought in Dave Gallatin, who I knew would be one of the most important members of the team. Gallatin had worked for me at Apple when we developed the second generation of the Newton Message Pad. Gallatin was one of the best product architects that I had ever encountered in Silicon Valley, and he had been a superstar at Apple. He was easy to work with, creative, hardworking, calm, and methodical, and always delivered on whatever he committed to. We had also worked together a few years earlier as part of the team that created the first Nook eBook reader for Barnes & Noble. Gallatin's expertise covered a wide area, including defining and designing the electronic hardware architecture and developing the product's firmware. Gallatin also had experience in designing some of the first non-phone products to use the Android operating system.

Also joining the team a few months later would be his business partner, Dave Paulsen, a veteran electronics engineer who had worked for many of the iconic hardware companies in Silicon Valley including Apple, Grid Computer, and NeXT. Paulsen had once run his own sixty-man electronic design company. He was the same engineer described in Isaacson's biography of Steve Jobs who had told the Apple chief what he could do with his job after Jobs insulted him and his team for only working eighty-hour weeks.

Last, we brought in a mechanical engineer, Simon Gatrall, who had once worked for IDEO but was then working independently. In addition, Jason Rubenstein, who had previously been working with Mark Goldstein on the Pono music store and the user interface for the player, continued in that role. Our audio expert would be Bob Stuart of Meridian.

PRODUCT GOAL

The goal was to build a small, affordable music player that could play back high-resolution audio files better than anything available on the market. It was to be simple to use and targeted to all those who loved to listen to music, but without the complexity found on existing products designed for audiophiles. Neil's goal was to expose a new generation of listeners, those who grew up listening to MP3 files, to something much better. He mentioned how his daughter, Amber, felt cheated when he explained to her that she was actually listening to a dumbed-down version of the original music, and he believed many others who had only been exposed to MP3 would feel the same way once they began using Pono.

We realized that this undertaking had a lot of risk. Not the risk of designing and building a player; that we knew we could do. The concern was with the current market trends and the market acceptance of a player. More and more music was being consumed, not as physical media, not as files on stand-alone music players or even phones, but as music streamed over the internet, delivered directly from the cloud. Apple's sales of iPods had begun to plateau and were expected to soon decline. And numerous companies were offering streaming music for just a few dollars per month or even free with ads. Streaming was the enemy of quality music, but it didn't seem to matter to the millions who listened to it in greater and greater numbers because of its convenience and low cost. We knew we were fighting an uphill battle but one that we believed would show how much better music could be.

Inspired by Neil's passion for what we were doing, we were all focused on our jobs and not worrying about what we couldn't control. It's easy to dwell on "what ifs," but our job was to design and build the superlative player that Neil had asked for.

THE MARKET

The market for music consisted mostly of low-end streaming that was very convenient but had mediocre quality; music players that played downloaded, compressed files such as the iPod; and music player apps built into smartphones that worked much the same way. The high-end audio industry was entirely different. It had been associated with hobbyists and the privileged few who were willing to search for their high-quality music and hardware, then assemble the best audio system that they could afford. Just the process of buying music from the existing high-res stores required knowledge of a half-dozen file types with cryptic names. It was sometimes hard to know which albums really were high res or if they had been modified to make them seem like they were higher quality than they really were. In other words, listening to high-quality audio took work.

MUSIC STORE

By contrast, in building the Pono player and our own accompanying high-resolution music store, we would provide a complete and affordable way to enjoy quality music. To make it as seamless as possible, the music store would sell content for download to a computer and transfer to the player. It would be much easier to use than existing stores and would focus on high res.

Neil wanted the store to be simple and easy to access for both finding and listening to quality music. It was a gift he wanted to give to all those who love listening to music, a segment he believed was much larger than the audiophile market.

While Neil was excited to move forward with the player and store, it was still not exactly his ideal solution. He ultimately envisioned that the music player would be synced to a tablet that would bring up details about the album as it was playing. The tablet would display lyrics, the history of the performance, contributors, and detailed liner notes about the performers. It would have been complicated to do and not something feasible at the time. But it would not be forgotten, because Neil had the vision and would somehow find a way to do it—if not now, then perhaps later.

Chapter 9 | Neil

PONO IS FOR AND BY THE ARTISTS

I wanted to create Pono as a way for my artist friends to fight back to protect their art, and they gave me a lot of their support and encouragement for doing it. They trusted me to speak for them, and many of them invested in the company and supported our Kickstarter campaign. I viewed Pono as a cause for artists, music lovers, and all of music. My goal was not to build a hardware company; other companies were a lot better and more experienced at that. This was much more, an example to show the industry what could be done to improve the quality of a listener's experience.

Some thought that because of the success of Beats headphones around the same time, I was trying to duplicate their model. But that was wrong, both based on what Beats was doing and what my goal was. Beats was never about music fidelity. They were about creating a mass-market product that used fashion and pumped the bass sound to market their headphones, and they did a great job at it. It worked for hip-hop and rap.

On the other hand, the Pono player was intended to address audio accuracy and to prove that there was an audience that could appreciate high-res music. Frank Sinatra's music did not need the bass to be pumped. I would give listeners a place to go to buy their music and a community where they could share their experiences with others. And by putting my name behind it, I wanted to move the conversation about high-resolution recordings beyond the audiophiles and into the mainstream. I knew it might be controversial in times when everyone thought the technology of cell phones was the answer to everything, but there needed to be more awareness of how good music could really be. It was not enough to just be able to recognize a song. You had to *feel* it.

We certainly weren't the first player. When we began Pono, there were a few other audio players on the market that played high-res files. However, they were either very expensive or not very good quality, or both. The most well-known brand was Astell&Kern, a Korean manufacturer that created high-res players for audiophiles. But at the time, they cost more than $1,000, with some models now costing around $3,500! I thought that made no sense because it made high res even more expensive to enjoy and made the musical experience only for the rich, who would be branded (along with high-resolution music) as elitists. That just advanced the message of the record companies—that high quality was something that had to cost much more and was out of reach for the average music lover. It was a losing proposition from the beginning.

Our goal was to create an affordable product that had no audio compromises and would be the best player for high-res tracks. We weren't quite sure how we'd accomplish that, but that was our goal.

At the same time, Pono had to offer what listeners of MP3 players had: ease of use, convenience, compatibility, and portability. I wanted Pono to become a movement for quality music, a movement for and on behalf of the music lovers and artists.

It was depressing to me that many of my artist friends were no longer recording their albums at the high quality they once did. The studios wanted to save a little money in their recording costs and the artists just didn't think about it or know better. With the fans not demanding the higher-quality music, there was no pressure on the record companies to produce it.

It wasn't just about new digital music. It was about the history of music, every recording that came before the digital age. The record labels possessed all of those original analog tape masters. It was their opportunity to save those masters by transferring them to high-resolution digital before they degraded as a result of time. There were thousands of these recordings and the cost of remastering would be astronomical. However, it seemed obvious to me that the solution was to start with the highest-selling albums, say the top 500. That meant that at $2,000 for each remastering process, the top 500 records could be done for a million dollars. Split among all of the record companies, that was not a very big deal. It would save for posterity the most popular records made before the dawn of digital. That *is* a big deal. As I'm writing this today, it has still not happened.

Why do the labels not want to save their crown jewels—the music of Elvis, Sinatra, Crosby, the whole big band era, Bob Dylan, Sarah Vaughan, Joan Baez, Lena Horne, Woody Guthrie, and many, many more? I can find no good answer.

DRM: WHERE GREED MEETS MUSIC

Another important decision we made was not to use any copy protection on the Pono music files that we would be selling. Music used to be protected using what was called "digital rights management" (DRM). It was a way to restrict how the files could be used and copied, and it caused a lot of problems, particularly for those who purchased the audio files. Artists hated this as well, because it reflected poorly on them and the whole industry.

In the end, DRM was a failed scheme. It led companies such as Napster to find ways around it, such as building sharing sites. And DRM made it more difficult for paying customers to enjoy their music whenever and wherever they wanted, because it limited their ability to play the recordings they bought on their different devices. They couldn't just copy it and add it to the other device like they could with a photo. DRM gave the industry a black eye because it hurt their paying customers most of all, treating them as criminals. As for stealing and copying, we have to live with it. Theft of property is part of the digital age. Thankfully, not everyone is a thief.

UNLIMITED PLAYBACK

In addition, I believed Pono music files should play on any device and not be limited to Pono players, unlike Apple files that used their own proprietary file format. I wanted to eliminate all of the roadblocks and restrictions the industry had erected between the music and the listener. I knew I was speaking for all the artists.

FLAC

I wanted the Pono music files to be the highest possible quality audio available anywhere. The industry-wide standard for lossless compression was FLAC—simply a digital-storage format that took the high-res digital file and reduced it in size by almost half but without any loss of the useful data. This compression does not kill the sound, as MP3 compression does. FLAC was also the most widely used format for lossless audio and could play on nearly everything. Whether the file was 192/24 or lower, we decided that everything on Pono would be in FLAC to make it accessible.

PROVENANCE

Pono audio files would be special in another way. We would guarantee that what we sold was authenticated to be at original quality and not an audio file that was artificially manipulated to appear to be at a higher resolution, something called upsampling.

I hired Bruce Botnick, a renowned audio engineer and old friend who had worked with me on Buffalo Springfield, to work with me to ensure the provenance of our content and to work with other artists, their managers, and recording companies to find new high-resolution content from their vaults. A Pono file would be seen as the trusted source for all high-resolution audio by labels and artists. That was our goal.

To signify that a file was authentic, Bob Stuart came up with the idea to put a blue light on the Pono player that would go on when a Pono recording was being played, letting the user know that the recording was Pono: the highest resolution, a pure, unaltered file.

Because the amount of music available in high res was still limited—only about 4,000 albums out of several million—I used both my and Elliot's relationships with artists and their managers to get more high-res content produced. We worked with them to find content that was recorded but unreleased in high res and bring that content into our music store. Sometimes we found that an album was only released in CD quality, and we'd go back to the studio masters and try to create a high-res version to sell on our site. We usually had to pay a recording engineer to transfer the original to a high-resolution digital file. Pono needed to pay that cost, because the recording companies had little interest in doing it themselves.

Unfortunately, the economics were not good. The cost of remastering was about $2,000 for each album. If we sold it for $15, the record companies got 70 percent and Pono would make $4.50. That meant we'd need to sell more than 400 downloads of each album just to break even, a big challenge for a startup company. In my mind, I thought the responsibility would live with the record companies. They did not see it that way.

Despite all the challenges, we decided to go ahead. I wanted to support the artists and for everyone to have a chance to experience their work the way it was meant to be heard. With that decision, I ventured financially much further out on a limb.

Chapter 10 | Phil

INVENTING PONO

By the spring of 2012, the development team was fully engaged in developing the Pono player. We would spend more than two years working together before the player began shipping to customers near the end of 2014. During that time, we faced numerous obstacles that would slow us down and even cause the work to stop for months at a time, such as running out of money, a succession of CEO candidates, and a few technical challenges.

In similar circumstances it might have caused team members to leave and look for a more stable situation, but that was never the case here. Uncertainty is a familiar situation in Silicon Valley. Some of us jumped onto other short-term projects while waiting, but we all continued to believe in the project's importance and, despite the ups and downs, setbacks, and financial challenges, we all loved what we were doing.

Managing the Pono team was much less of a challenge than with previous projects I've worked on, because its members had been selected specifically for their particular skills. All were smart, professional, highly motivated, and excited to be working with Neil. It was one the best product development teams I've ever worked with.

I've usually found that working with a small, smart development team is much more effective than working with a large product design organization, particularly when you can build that team with engineers matched to the exact needs of the product being developed. The other benefits are that the development cost is lower, it takes less time, and the resulting product is usually better designed.

TONE AT THE TOP

The other element that's important to an effective development effort is the tone that's set at the top; it can make or break a project. I've worked in organizations with leadership that could demotivate an entire team, set back progress, create chaos, and cause high turnover. That can happen when the leader has unrealistic expectations or no understanding of product development, which, by its nature, is filled with uncertainty and risk. In the case of this project, it was just the opposite. Even though this was the biggest product development effort Neil had ever been involved with, to the team he was always positive, appreciative, and highly motivating.

Initially, I didn't know what to expect when I began working with Neil. Often, you'll hear about a famous personality that has one persona as their public face and a quite different one when they're out of the limelight. How would Neil react to problems? Would he be impatient like other managers I've worked with, or would he be like he was in public?

Fortunately, the real Neil was much like his public persona. Calm, polite, smart, and a great listener. He set high expectations and big goals, but he wanted to learn as much as he could about what we were doing. He was highly inquisitive; he was hands on when he needed to be, but he always had a clear vision of the product's big picture and his mission. Most importantly, he showed the same respect to each team member as they showed to him. Neil would occasionally dismiss his own skills as a CEO, but he showed a truly natural ability to be an incredibly effective leader.

Neil's approach made a huge difference. While it didn't relieve any pressure, it did make the project challenging, stimulating, and a lot of fun. We all wanted to please him and do our best. For me it meant working harder than I had ever done before on any product and under more pressure than I had ever experienced. While that pressure was completely self-imposed, I kept thinking that I just couldn't disappoint Neil or do anything to damage his reputation. Ironically, his own reputation was never much of a concern to Neil and seemed to be the last thing on his mind. But because Neil's Pono initiative was so visible, a result of the numerous rumors and speculative articles in the press, I felt that added pressure to deliver. I would often think late at night about the impact of things going wrong. I made it harder on myself than it needed to be. But I was juggling scores of issues in my mind about every aspect of the product and I was all-consumed with it.

While this was Neil's first development effort of this magnitude, I learned that he has a history of inventing, building products, and immersing himself in technology. Years earlier, his interest in model railroading led to his developing an advanced wireless control system called TrainMaster, a remote mobile device that controlled the trains, switch tracks, and accessories—a product much more advanced than anything else available. He even created an early website under the pseudonym of Clyde Coil (http://coilcouplers.com/tmc/tmc.html).

Neil understood the basic design process and was interested in the details, particularly relating to the customer's experience and all things that would affect audio quality. He would lead our monthly meetings at his ranch, where we'd cover the progress, issues, and decisions that needed to be made since we had last met. The meetings would last for three or four hours and were very productive. We'd also get updates on management issues from Elliot and from Bob Stuart on his developing technology.

BEGINNING THE DESIGN

The design efforts began by first defining the basic requirements of the Pono player from the perspective of the customer. This included the major features of the product, such as the touch display, buttons, memory, connectors, battery life, and audio capabilities. The team began with the industrial design (ID) that Mike Nuttall, working with Mark Goldstein, had developed, a triangular shape resembling a Toblerone candy bar. The ID was one of the most controversial aspects but was one I thought to be well conceived, not only aesthetically but also functionally.

The ID process begins once the major functional components needed for the product are defined. The industrial designer then determines the physical arrangement of the components that would result in an attractive and functional form factor so that all the user-facing elements are in suitable locations—in this case, the display, control buttons, connectors, and charge ports. The resulting design needs to be manufacturable and usable in a variety of ways: in the hand, in the pocket, on a desk, and in an automobile.

To create a design that didn't compromise the audio quality, we required some large components that were not normally used in portable players. While the most obvious shape would have been a flat rectangle, much like a smartphone or iPod, these large parts wouldn't fit.

The triangular shape allowed us to fit in the large output capacitors used in the amplification stage, along with a long cylindrical battery that fit along one of the edges. That was consistent with our decision not to make any compromises to the audio quality by limiting the size of the components. At this early stage, we had little idea of the power requirements, so we wanted to use the largest and most efficiently-shaped battery possible, a cylinder. Thus, the ID was as much form following function as function following form. The triangular form was one of the Pono player's special attributes and something Mike and Neil liked from the beginning.

It could sit on a desk or atop your sound system with its tilted display or fit comfortably in the hand with the screen held vertically, and easily slip into most pockets. We expected the shape of Pono to be somewhat polarizing, much like other iconic designs, and it was.

ELECTRONICS DESIGN

Designing the electronics was the most complex and time-consuming part, compared to the more straightforward mechanical design. Dave Gallatin, our electronics engineer, went to work selecting the operating system and processor, essential elements to the product's overall design architecture, performance, and cost. Too powerful a processor would shorten battery life and be more expensive, but too weak a processor would slow down performance, such as loading files. He settled on a processor from Texas Instruments and the Android operating system. Android provided many of the requirements we needed, such as controlling a touch display, power management, and a user interface.

While used mostly in phones at the time, Android was a freely available operating system that's now used in a variety of non-phone products. Pono would not look or work like a phone, but it would have an interface that worked much like a phone app. Using a mature operating system would save development time.

AUDIO

Neil was heavily involved in the product definition and decisions, particularly in the shape, color, controls, and touch display. When the subject turned to audio features, such as adding an equalizer that would alter the sound characteristics, Neil's influence was strongly felt. He was particularly opposed to features that manipulated the music, such as boosting the bass, altering the frequency response, or creating artificial effects. These features would take away from the authenticity of the sound and change what the artist had created and intended. They would get in the way, in between the original performance and the listener, just as compressed audio files got in the way. They would also add complications to using the player, and that was not what Pono was about.

The design progressed from a concept to a series of breadboards: handmade models that would allow us to listen to music, start testing the various features, and provide a means for developing and testing the software.

As the first pass of the mechanical and electrical designs was nearing completion, we began doing internal testing to identify issues and make refinements. Product development is the process of designing, testing, improving the design, and testing again, each time getting closer to the final product. At this point, the prototypes didn't look anything like a real product; they were just a mishmash of circuit boards, wires, and loose components.

Originally, Mike Nuttall wanted the housing to be made of extruded aluminum with the electronics, battery, and display designed to slide in from one end, captured and sealed using end caps, much like a ship in a bottle. That would provide an elegant housing with no visible seams or fasteners. Mike and Neil specifically didn't want the seam between the sections of the case to be felt when held in the hand. But that approach was too difficult to implement and added a lot of complexity. Ultimately, we went to a two-piece plastic housing that would snap together and be reinforced with silicone adhesive. By moving the seam away from the edges of the housing toward the back, we eliminated it from being felt when holding the player.

Since we wanted no screws to be used to assemble the case, for aesthetic reasons, Simon, our mechanical engineer, recommended that the two parts of the enclosure be sealed with a permanent adhesive in order to prevent it from opening if dropped. The normal requirement for a portable consumer product such as the Pono is that it withstand a three-foot drop onto a hardwood floor, and he didn't think we'd pass otherwise.

I thought passing the drop test was less important than repairability; permanently gluing the two halves together would make it impossible to diagnose and repair the product after it was assembled, and it would make recycling at the end of the product's life more difficult. I also knew Neil would never accept a product that would adversely affect the environment. There are few more attuned and sensitive to environmental issues than Neil. As it turned out, because of an unexpected event, this decision would have a huge impact later on, when we were ready to ship.

As we progressed with the design, we began tooling the plastic parts to be able to produce them in volume, and continued to refine the circuit boards, with the goal of building a couple of dozen working prototypes in January 2013.

DAVID LETTERMAN SHOW

But in early September, I received a call from Elliot telling me that Neil was going to be a guest on *The Late Show with David Letterman* in a few weeks and that Neil wanted to show Pono.

Up to that time, no one outside of the company knew any of the specifics about Pono, just that Neil spoke about it frequently. Although we were months from building our first device that actually looked like Pono, this was a unique opportunity for Neil to explain more about it and what it stood for. Millions of people would be introduced to a product we were working on.

I discussed the opportunity with the development team and we came up with an idea. We'd build a nonworking model using a machined plastic housing and fit it with a battery, an LED, and diffuser that would rear-illuminate a color transparency of the Pono's home screen. It would have a switch on the back to turn on the light.

We quickly built the device and gave it to Neil. When he appeared on *The Late Show* on September 27, 2012,[6] and Letterman asked about Pono, Neil pulled the jury-rigged device from his pocket and held it up to the camera, flipping the light on at the same time. It looked just like a real Pono. That was how the world first learned what Pono was all about. Neil did not represent it as a fully operating device, instead calling it a looks-like model, but for all practical purposes it looked real and much like the product we would ship.

---

6   "Neil Young al David Letterman Show del 27-9-12," YouTube video, 4:08, posted by "Neil Young provincia di Milano," September 30, 2012, https://www.youtube.com/watch?v=qL1ffo8TwGM.

FIRST PROTOTYPES

In January, we built our first twenty-five looks-like units that really did work. For the first time we would have something we could hold in our hands and use. I visited the small prototype factory in Fremont, California, where Dave Paulsen was assembling the first units by hand. One by one, in eager anticipation, he'd power them up and see if they worked. Some did, and some didn't. Those that worked would be put to one side and those that didn't would go to an area to be debugged. The problems were generally minor, a bad solder connection or a missing part. These development validation test (DVT) units would significantly accelerate our progress. Some would be used to develop and test software, others were used for creating firmware (software permanently in the player's memory), and still others would be used to fine-tune the mechanical design. For the first time we could imagine the product going into production. It was becoming more real than ever.

MISSING IN ACTION

But these Pono DVT units were missing one important element: the compression software that Bob Stuart had promised. In meeting after meeting, Stuart had explained that still more work was needed on his software but assured us it was coming soon.

Not having this software on hand was slowing our progress. It was this feature that we believed to be key to making the player unique and something that would help us raise more funding. Stuart's software would let our player hold more high-res files in less memory. Instead, the Pono DVT units had a generic music player design that Dave Gallatin built. We were excited to have our first players, and the audio performance sounded very good, but without Stuart's software there was nothing unique about the audio design.

Chapter 11 | Phil

LEADERSHIP AT PONO

A great product idea is certainly not enough to be successful. The product idea is usually the easiest part of building a product company. You also need sufficient funding and experienced management. My job at that time was developing the hardware, so I had limited interaction with the board of directors other than providing regular updates on the progress of the Pono player. But there was a lot going on behind the scenes.

BOARD OF DIRECTORS

Pono had a board of directors that was based on friendships, relationships, and personal recommendations, much the way many boards in small companies are formed. But few among this group were experienced in building and running a Silicon Valley startup.

The board consisted of the late Pegi Young, Elliot Roberts, Gigi Brisson, John Tyson, and Neil. Pegi was Neil's then-wife, and Elliot was his friend and manager. Brisson was an investor and neighbor of Neil's in Hawaii, and Tyson was a close and trusted friend of Neil's and the board member with the most experience, from running his family's business, Tyson Foods. Rick Cohen, a corporate lawyer with the law firm Buchalter in Los Angeles, attended board meetings as legal counsel for the company. Collectively, they had limited experience with high-tech startups.

MANAGEMENT

Elliot also served as Pono's COO. He was a great manager and businessman with legendary experience in the music business. Early in his career, he had run a record company with David Geffen and was introduced to Neil by Joni Mitchell, one of his clients at the time.

While Neil began as Pono's CEO, it was clear to him and to Elliot that the company needed a full-time leader with experience in building and running a startup, and most importantly, someone who could bring in more funding. Developing a new hardware product, even with a lean team, was costly and all-consuming.

EARLY INVESTORS

Financing to that point was mostly from Neil, Tyson, Neil's artist friends, and a number of private investors, totaling a few million dollars. They invested because they believed in what Neil was doing and wanted to support his efforts.

Often, Elliot would express his surprise and frustration to me about how expensive it was to develop hardware. That was not unexpected because he and Neil had little experience in this area. Most companies that get into the hardware business for the first time have the same reaction. Hardware is expensive to design, build, and manufacture. In retrospect, I should have been more proactive by developing a more detailed development budget. Instead, I assumed that the money would follow as we crossed each development milestone. That pointed out another management deficiency we had—no CFO, resulting in a lack of accurate forecasting. Naively, I just assumed that Neil could bring in the funding we needed.

FINDING A NEW CEO

While Neil and Elliot took on the roles of CEO and COO, Neil also had his job as an active musician and Elliot continued to manage Neil's career with a small staff in a downtown Santa Monica office.

Neil was constantly busy writing, recording, and promoting his new albums and left town for extended periods on worldwide concert tours. He was also writing his autobiography and had a few other projects on the side. Neil very badly wanted a CEO to take some of the load off his shoulders and to build the company, someone more experienced than himself.

Finding that person turned out to be a difficult effort that stretched for more than a year. I assumed it would be much easier than it turned out to be, but, in fact, it was difficult to find someone who felt the same way that Neil did about his mission. Although we read so much about the risk taking among Silicon Valley executives, we saw little of that among the potential candidates that came by. It didn't help that the company was not well funded, which would limit what a new CEO could do in their first days. In fact, the new CEO's first job would be to find money.

I had recommended to Neil and Elliot that they hire an experienced search person to find a candidate, but they and the board preferred to rely on personal recommendations and avoid that expense.

Pono went through a few trial candidates, those that Elliot would encourage to come in as a consultant and try to raise some funding as one of their first jobs. Some of the candidates liked the idea of working with Neil, but many wanted to run their own show. It was one of the few times where Neil's involvement in the company made it more difficult to do something. While Neil's association with Pono was important, it also attracted unqualified candidates and lookers who were more interested in the association with Neil than in the hard work the job entailed.

One candidate joined and, on paper, seemed promising. He had experience in the streaming music area and was well connected to the industry. But in short order he tried to recast all of Neil's efforts in his own vision, including wanting to stop the Pono development and outsource it to another company that he had a relationship with, but that had little product experience of this type. He then announced on social media, to several board members' horror, that he and Neil had just founded a new company together. He didn't last long after that!

Eventually, a CEO was found. John Hamm was hired in April 2013. He came to us because of a chance meeting between his wife and Gigi Brisson at a TED conference in San Francisco. Hamm had the ideal background, with experience as an investor, board member, and management advisor to several startup and established technology companies. He also had a strong interest and involvement in music, as an audiophile and a board member of the Grammy Foundation.

John Hamm with Neil

He complemented Neil's skills with his own experience in building companies, raising money, and understanding music, marketing, and corporate governance. Hamm shared Neil's beliefs about the pursuit of quality audio. He also brought credibility that could help with potential investors and had plenty of experience in raising money for cash-strapped companies such as ours. In addition, he was smart, charismatic, high energy, and personable.

Hamm articulated his thoughts well as soon as he joined:

> *The force of Neil's will was an inflection point. Every time there's a brewing grassroots movement, it always takes someone of stature to put their body on the front line. A lot of people*

talked the game of better audio, but Neil was the only one to put his badge on the table and lay across the tracks. Neil was willing to use his position in the industry to call attention to as much the shitty quality of MP3 as the great quality of studio masters.

He pointed out how bad MP3 is as a representation of an artist's intention and to really expose that. What an insulting technical format it was to the effort artists put into their recordings. I remember when we were shooting video driving around Mulholland Drive and talking about the laborious task of making a record. The time it took to get a mic just right on a drum, the numbers of remixes, the work that engineers and producers would do. The fact that all of that is then substantially degraded by the format of playback. It would be like taking an artist's picture and making a blurry copy.

Hamm's business skills were a strong complement to Neil's vision. The expectation was that Hamm could at last turn Neil's vision into a business that could succeed and be successfully funded. It seemed like we had the perfect duo.

GETTING REAL

Hamm jumped right in and began to put into place the structure of a serious Silicon Valley startup company. We started meeting regularly at his San Francisco home to identify the resources we needed. We developed a budget and a detailed schedule that covered every key milestone to commercialization for each critical element: the player, the music store, manufacturing, and marketing. Hamm formalized my role as vice president of hardware and operations and expressed confidence that he could raise the needed money to bring on the additional resources we were lacking.

With the work on the music download store languishing and the scope of what was needed growing in complexity compared to what we'd originally assumed, Hamm recruited a vice president of technology, Pedram Abrari, the software counterpart to my position in hardware. Abrari had experience developing cloud-based software products and was a strong addition to the company. Abrari, in turn, hired a software design engineer, a software quality engineer, and an engineer with experience in building online stores.

Hamm also hired a business development manager, Randy Leasure, and a marketing director, Sami Kamangar (Pedram's spouse). Considering the scope of our undertaking, we still had a relatively small group—fewer than ten full-time employees in addition to four consultants on the hardware team.

Hamm leased an office on the third floor of a small office building in the Potrero Hill area of San Francisco, where we could all work together. The office consisted of a large open area with desks and tables, and a small room next door, our listening room for testing and demoing Pono.

With the additional employees and our first office, we were a real company and our development progress accelerated. The elements of an online music store were defined, and intensive work on it began. The store had many complexities to it. Not only did it need an online storefront that was visible to the customer for searching, selecting, and purchasing music, it also needed a complex behind-the-scenes infrastructure to manage the music library, download the music, and conduct the financial transactions with the record companies and our customers. Last, we needed applications for both Mac and Windows—much like iTunes—for users to manage their music files and load them onto the player.

Kevin Fielding, our new software engineer, quickly created a much-improved user interface for the player, and Damani Jackson, our software quality engineer, worked full-time testing it on the new players we had built. Irina Boykova was responsible for building the online store, while Zeke Young, Neil's son, focused on music content. Pono was becoming more real.

The Pono team: Irina Boykova, Dave Gallatin, Randy Leasure, Kevin Fielding, Dave Paulsen, Neil Young, Zeke Young, Sami Kamangar, Damani Jackson, Pedram Abrari, and Phil Baker

STILL MISSING IN ACTION

But late in 2013, a few months after Hamm arrived, we still faced a major issue: Bob Stuart still had not delivered his software that was to be incorporated into the player, the software designed to compress files to use less memory while retaining high-resolution sound. Making it available was part of an early agreement between Stuart and Pono in exchange for a sizable chunk of equity. But, as I later learned, the agreement was written in very general terms and failed to define the software with any precision. That probably made sense considering the agreement was written before we all really understood the specifics of the product we were to build, but Neil and Elliot wanted something formal in writing.

Stuart had been attending our monthly development meetings at Neil's ranch as the team's audio expert. But as we progressed with the development of the player, it was Gallatin who designed the player's electronics, while Stuart provided suggestions and comments along the way. Stuart's main contribution was to be his software.

In these meetings Stuart would describe his software in general terms with little specificity. He explained it as something very complex that involved encoding and decoding using both software and hardware. But he was always reluctant to provide specific details about when we'd see it.

I could sense that Neil was becoming frustrated and impatient, because that software was critical to completing and testing the player. It was not only Neil; the entire development team had begun to wonder whether we'd ever see anything. It made us all very nervous.

To keep moving forward, Gallatin added a programmable memory chip to the circuit of the Pono hardware design so that the software could be added after the player was built and bypassed in the meantime.

But we never received the software. I didn't know if Stuart's technology was not ready or if he was reluctant to provide it to us. I kept thinking that this was not the way a partner with equity should be behaving, but there was little I could do.

Finally, in our November monthly meeting, Stuart said he was ready to discuss the terms for Pono using the software. Hamm flew to the UK to meet with him and the investors in Meridian: the Richemont Group, a Switzerland-based company that owns a number of European luxury fashion brands.

The terms they proposed to Hamm included monthly payments, royalties for each player sold, more stock, and no exclusivity. The terms were much more onerous than Pono could afford and made no business sense based on normal industry standards. Not only would the software not be exclusive to Pono, but it also restricted what Pono could do with it. For example, if Pono was sold or licensed its player to be built or sold by another company, then his technology could not be included.

During these negotiations, Hamm explained our economics and tried to negotiate a more favorable arrangement. Discussions and negotiations continued for several months and included Hamm, Elliot, Neil, Cohen, and Stuart and his investors, but they never were able to come to an agreement.

When I interviewed Stuart for this book, he thought that Pono management had been unreasonable by not accepting his terms, because of the value his software would provide. Stuart felt its value was much greater than what Pono believed it to be. Stuart's software eventually became the basis for a proprietary compression technology called MQA.

This turn of events was a huge disappointment and a serious blow. Stuart had worked closely with us for two years, since the beginning of Pono's development, and we assumed he would provide this technology with terms we could all agree on. With my responsibility for getting the player designed, built, and tested, I was quite frustrated that this key element was unavailable while the players were otherwise completed.

This development could not have come at a worse time. It was late in 2013 and Hamm was working on bringing in outside investments, and one of the selling points of Pono was that it had this special technology that set it apart. While the Pono player would still work without Stuart's software, it would have little to distinguish it from other players. Moreover, it was important that Pono meet the high expectations Neil had set for it. It needed a distinguishing feature to differentiate it beyond Neil's involvement. We all were disappointed and wondered whether this would mean the end of Pono.

Meanwhile, the engineering for the Pono player had been completed, except for Stuart's software. We decided to plow forward and complete the build of the next fifty players without it, incorporating all of the design improvements we had been working on since we built the first group of players. They'd be far from perfect but would be a major milestone, allowing us to put players in the hands of Neil, the board, and others for testing.

Chapter 12 | Phil

A NEW DIRECTION

*D*espite the setback of losing Stuart's technology, we were not about to give up. We had come so far, and we weren't going to let this obstacle get in the way. Hamm began calling his many contacts in the audiophile community, asking them if they knew of another technology or audio expert who might have something that could help us distinguish the player. While no one was doing anything similar to what Stuart had been working on, Hamm was referred to Charley Hansen, the founder of Ayre Acoustics in Boulder, Colorado.

CHARLEY HANSEN

Charley was a brilliant designer of high-end audio equipment, including amplifiers, pre-amps, DACs, and other electronic components that were among the finest available in the world, with some components retailing for as much as $10,000.

He was passionate about audio quality, a real genius, and a contrarian about how audio products were being designed and marketed. In particular, he was critical about how most hardware manufacturers focused more on specs than audio quality. Charley obsessed about his product details, including features others ignored, such as the design and behavior of the volume control. He would fine-tune his designs by spending hours conducting listening tests as he made the tiniest changes to optimize the sound. Charley had been paralyzed below the chest after a motorcycle struck him head-on while bicycling years earlier and used a wheelchair. But he had kept applying his brilliant mind to building outstanding audio hardware.

When Hamm went to Boulder to meet with Charley, he asked if he'd be interested in working on Pono with Neil, and Charley became very excited. He told Hamm that he had always wanted to create an affordable listening device that tapped his expertise, and he thought he knew just what to do.

Charley dismissed Stuart's technology as solving a problem that didn't exist and therefore no longer needed solving. We had no reason to shrink the files at all, since memory and file size were not the issues they had been years earlier. Like Neil, he was opposed to a new proprietary music format that added new restrictions to the music files and was controlled by for-profit companies.

The key to designing an exceptional player, he explained, was to focus on improving the audio quality, which, he surmised, could be much better than anything now available. He would use one of the best DACs and incorporate a much better amplifier, based on the designs he used in his own high-end products.

He said he would pick the very best low-power DAC made for portable devices, and for the amplifier, use discrete components instead of off-the-shelf amplifier chips used in other players—again, what Charley did with his own audiophile products. The amplification design, he asserted, is one of the most important areas that impacts audio quality, and most companies get it all wrong.

While it might require hundreds of separate parts, including resistors, transistors, and capacitors, instead of a single inexpensive amplifier chip that everyone else used, Charley promised the performance would be much better than any other player ever made. It would be designed with no feedback loop, just as he designed his own products. Conventional products use a feedback loop that measures the output signal to adjust the input signal, something that he found degrades audio quality. Charley would also use a balanced output design, something only high-end audio products use, that provides two channels of audio, each through its own headphone jack, that are isolated from each other to deliver superior audio.

Charley confidently predicted

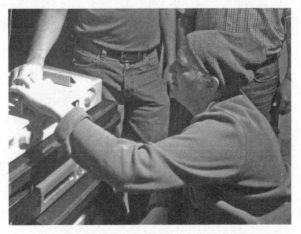

Charley Hansen, founder of Ayre Acoustics

he could create the best player that ever existed, and he was ready to get started.

We signed an agreement in which he would receive a royalty for each player sold, and Charley went to work. Charley's approach would require a redesign to a major portion of the Pono player's electronics and expert skills in being able to pack all the additional components onto the small circuit board. Dave Paulsen had just those skills, and he and Charley would work together for many months. Charley and Dave considered each other geniuses, because each was the best at what he did.

UNCERTAINTY

While we were elated that Charley had a solution, there were still lots of unknowns. Could we fit his new electronics into the player? What would it do to battery life? Could Charley really do what he promised?

If we could pull this off, it would be a great example of benefiting from a setback. We'd have a product that sounded better than anything we imagined, while losing a feature that wasn't nearly as useful as we had first assumed. After all, what would be preferable, a player that could hold more files, or a player that, in Neil's words, *sounded like God*?

The future became a little brighter as we moved into 2014. We had a strong CEO, capable teams hard at work on the player and the music store, and a new audio partner who could help us make the best portable player in the world.

However, we were still struggling to bring in enough money to fund the increase in activity. We continued to bring in small private investments, but few major ones. Yet, the need for cash would become even greater as we moved closer to manufacturing.

Hot Dusty Roads (stereo)

BURNED

Burned (mono)

OUT OF MY MIND

Out Of My Mind (mono)

Burned (stereo)

Out Of My Mind (stereo)

Kahuna Sunset

Kahuna Sunset

Down Down Down

Baby Don't Scold Me (mono)

Baby Don't Scold Me (stereo)

Down Down Down

FLYING ON THE GROUND

Flying On The Ground Is Wrong (mono)

Flying On The Ground Is Wrong (stereo)

For What It's Worth

For What It's Worth (mono)

1963

JAN | FEB | MAR | APR | MAY | JUN | JUL | AUG | SEP | OCT | NOV | DEC

NY Forms The Squires
Dec 1962

SQUIRES

- Compact cassette introduced
  Aug 30, 1963
- Rev. Martin Luther King Jr.'s
  "I have a dream" speech, Aug
- John F
  Nov 2

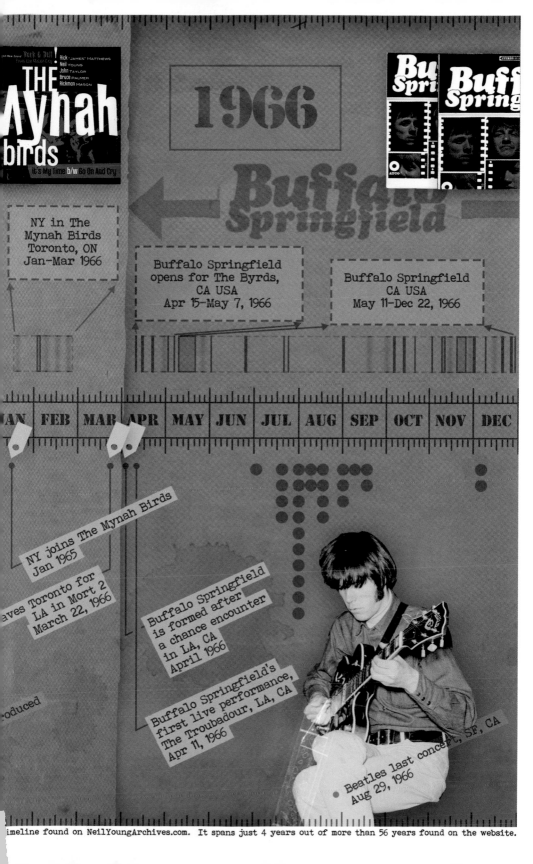

THE **Mynah** birds

Rick "JAMES" Matthews
Neil Young
John Taylor
Bruce Palmer
Rickman Mason

It's My Time! b/w Go On And Cry

1966

Buffalo Springfield

NY in The
Mynah Birds
Toronto, ON
Jan-Mar 1966

Buffalo Springfield
opens for The Byrds,
CA USA
Apr 15–May 7, 1966

Buffalo Springfield
CA USA
May 11–Dec 22, 1966

| JAN | FEB | MAR | APR | MAY | JUN | JUL | AUG | SEP | OCT | NOV | DEC |

NY joins The Mynah Birds
Jan 1965

...aves Toronto for
LA in Mort 2
March 22, 1966

Buffalo Springfield
is formed after
a chance encounter
in LA, CA
April 1966

...roduced

Buffalo Springfield's
first live performance,
The Troubadour, LA, CA
Apr 11, 1966

Beatles last concert, SF, CA
Aug 29, 1966

I Ain't Got The Blues

Nowadays Clancy Can't Even Sing

Runaround Babe

The Ballad Of Peggy Grover

The Rent Is Always Due

Extra, Extra

It's My Time

Go On And Cry

FLYING ON THE GROUND

NOWADAYS CLANCY CANTEVEN SING

The Archives Vol. 1 Disc 0 Early Years (1963–1965)

"It's My Time" b/w "Go On And Cry"

It's My Time

Go On And Cry

Flying On The Ground Is Wrong

Nowadays Clancy Can't Even Sing (mono)

Go nd Can Goodbye

than 56 years found on the website.

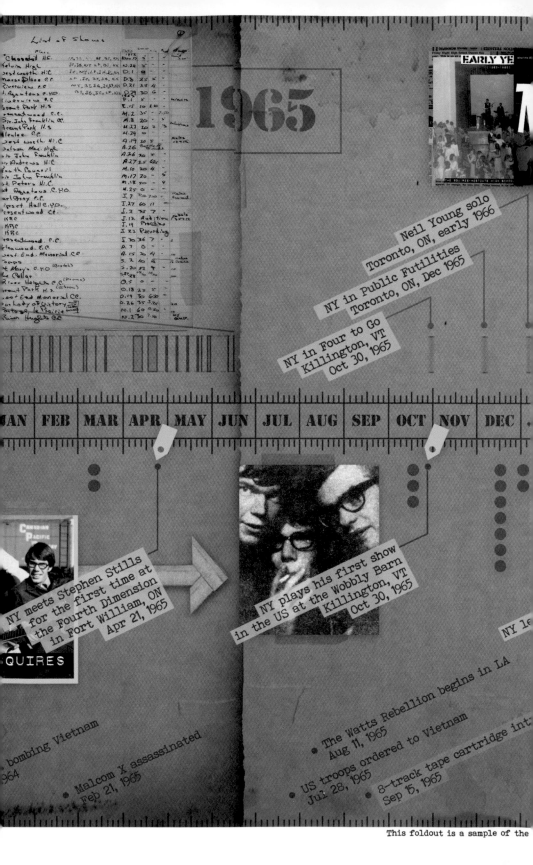

List of Shows

1965

Neil Young solo
Toronto, ON, early 1966

NY in Public Futilities
Toronto, ON, Dec 1965

NY in Four to Go
Killington, VT
Oct 30, 1965

| JAN | FEB | MAR | APR | MAY | JUN | JUL | AUG | SEP | OCT | NOV | DEC |

SQUIRES

NY meets Stephen Stills
for the first time at
the Fourth Dimension
in Fort William, ON
Apr 21, 1965

NY plays his first show
in the US at the Wobbly Barn
Killington, VT
Oct 30, 1965

NY le

bombing Vietnam
964

Malcom X assassinated
Feb 21, 1965

The Watts Rebellion begins in LA
Aug 11, 1965

US troops ordered to Vietnam
Jul 28, 1965

8-track tape cartridge int
Sep 15, 1965

This foldout is a sample of the

1964

NY in The Squires
Canada
Feb 1963–Jun 1965

| JAN | FEB | MAR | APR | MAY | JUN | JUL | AUG | SEP | OCT | NOV | DEC |

SQUIRES

28, 1963

Kennedy assassinated
1963

Civil Rights Act of 1964
July 2, 1964

Gulf of Tonkin incident
Aug 2, 1964

US beg
Nov 2

Go And Say Goodbye (stereo)

Nowadays Clancy Can't Even Sing (stereo)

Sit Down I Think I Love You (mono)

Hot Dusty Roads (mono)

Everybody's Wrong (mono)

Do I Have To Come Right Out And Say It (mono)

Leave (mono)

Leave (stereo)

Sit Down I Think I Love You (stereo)

Pay The Price (mono)

Everybody's Wrong (stereo)

Do I Have To Come Right Out And Say It (stereo)

Pay The Price (stereo)

Chapter 13 | Phil

OUR KICKSTARTER ADVENTURE

With the continuing difficulty we had in raising funding, the idea of doing a Kickstarter campaign became more appealing. It was something that we had discussed over the previous six months but never actively pursued. It had always been a consideration, mostly in the back of our minds, to be used much like the fire alarm on the wall with the inscription "Pull Lever in Case of Emergency." That time had arrived.

Up to this point, we all had been working under a lot of pressure to complete the basic design of the player. We reached a point in the development where we had built fifty prototypes for testing. It was the first time we had a "looks like, almost works like" product to hold in our hands. While it didn't have Stuart's software or the new electronic design that Charley Hansen was developing, it allowed us to test almost everything else. It was a major milestone, one of the most exciting times in the development of a new product, when you go from having a few rough prototypes to dozens of identical-looking units that are close to the finished product.

No one was more excited than Neil to get one in his hands. He used it day and night, and over the next few months became the most prolific of all those testing the player. He'd find all the issues and bugs before any of us and would suggest many improvements, particularly for the software and user interface. While sometimes it would be embarrassing that he found a bug first, we all were resigned to the fact that he was just better than any of us in discovering issues. It was the same characteristic we saw over and over in Neil, doing everything with a high degree of passion and being a perfectionist about whatever project he took on.

SERIOUS NEED FOR MONEY

Focusing on the players, however, masked our serious financial state. We had managed to survive with financing from Neil's friends and many small investors who believed in Neil's cause. But we all knew that now, to get any further and take Pono into production, we would require much more money.

Designing hardware products is an expensive process. The development costs are rarely predictable, with the need to design, test, and redesign many times over to get everything working correctly. But the largest expense is purchasing the parts needed to build production quantities of the product well in advance of being able to sell them. The amount can be more than all the previous costs combined. This is the point that many startup companies reach, only to realize they need much more money than they anticipated. They're suddenly surprised, unable to raise the needed funding to proceed, and often stall or even go out of business. It's also the time when companies examine their product and sometimes cancel it if the market has changed and their product is no longer competitive. It's the point of no return because these costs can typically reach a few million dollars. We were fast approaching this critical milestone as the new design was nearing completion.

With Stuart's technology off the table and Hansen's still an unproven alternative, there was too much doubt and uncertainty, at least among the large professional investors. Some still believed that no one cared about high-res music. Others believed streaming was replacing downloads and our approach was too little, too late. And some just didn't want to invest in a company headed by a rock star. Neil was undeterred and did a couple of private concerts to bring in enough money to keep us going.

KICKING OFF KICKSTARTER

Kickstarter now looked like our best option. We debated how a Kickstarter campaign would affect Neil's image. It was rare at the time for successful artists to appeal to the public to raise money, when the public's perception was that artists could fund a project on their own—a perception not always consistent with reality.

Neil lived modestly, for the most part, but had huge expenses associated with supporting his family and his staff. The investments he kept putting into Pono were more to support the cause of music than to make a lot of money. He had much better ways to make money than working so hard on Pono. This was a labor of love. He kept pouring in money until his financial advisor told him, no more.

In January we decided to proceed with a Kickstarter campaign. In addition to providing us the money we needed to continue, we thought it would answer, once and for all, whether people really cared about high-quality audio. The professional investors we met with had dismissed the need for better audio and said no one cared anymore. Kickstarter could prove them wrong.

A Kickstarter campaign is simple in concept. It asks individuals to pledge a dollar amount in return for the expectation of receiving a reward—in our case, a Pono music player. Technically, it's not a purchase but a donation. The donor hopes they'll get what was offered, but there's no assurance that they'll get anything. There's no recourse and no refunds, because they've not bought anything. If the campaign fails to reach its goal, then the money is returned. That encourages companies not to set too high of a goal, but it also means some companies make their goal but don't have enough money to fulfill their commitments.

If a campaign reaches its goal after concluding, the company receives a lump sum payment, minus a commission to Kickstarter and payment processing fees to Amazon, together totaling about 10 percent of the gross.

At the time, in early 2014, few Kickstarter campaigns had raised large amounts of money. The biggest success had been the Pebble Watch, a watch connected to a phone that was the precursor to the Apple Watch and that raised more than $10 million—an astonishing amount. Most Kickstarter campaigns brought in anywhere from tens of thousands of dollars to, in rare cases, a few hundred thousand.

While many of us kept analyzing and discussing whether we should do Kickstarter, Neil was the most comfortable with just going forward and doing it. As was his nature, Neil often came to his conclusions based on intuition and instinct, doing what was best for his fans, fellow musicians, and music itself. While many of us were worried about his reputation as a result of doing Kickstarter, that was never an issue with Neil. When he believed in something, he pushed forward and never seemed to worry how others judged him. If something didn't work, there was always plan B. He rarely looked back to express regrets.

Because the project was backed by Neil Young, we got the attention of Kickstarter's cofounder Yancey Strickler, who encouraged us to move forward but counseled us to ask for less than a million dollars, explaining that a celebrity asking for so much money might result in a backlash that would hurt the campaign and tarnish the celebrity's reputation.

Kickstarter recommends that campaigns begin before the product is completed, but usually within six to nine months of when it's expected to be done. That adds to the excitement and creates more interest around the campaign. At the time of our offering, fewer than a quarter of the campaigns that were funded were successful as measured by the donor receiving what they pledged for, and many of those that were successful took years longer than promised.

In addition to getting the needed cash, Kickstarter can help measure interest in a product—still a big question we had. While we all cared deeply and believed our mission was important to music and the artists, how did others feel? While not scientific, a good showing on Kickstarter would confirm interest and might encourage others to invest. The big fear of those doing Kickstarter campaigns is to not reach their goal and, consequently, having to return the contributions, facing the disappointment of not enough interest, and even closing down.

Our Kickstarter campaign promise was to deliver a Pono music player, which still was being designed. We didn't know how long that would take or how much the final product would cost. We didn't even know whether Charley's new design would fit into the case or how well it would work; we only had the promise from Hansen that he could do something that would sound great. That didn't stop us from showing our current test models on our Kickstarter website. The fact that we were able to show many details gave us credibility that we were real and had a good chance of doing what we said we could.

To help us design and promote the Kickstarter campaign, we enlisted Alex Daly, a Brooklyn-based consultant who had run several successful Kickstarter campaigns and who a few years later become known as the "Crowdsourceress" after publishing a book by that name. Her task was to develop enticing content for the Kickstarter site and define all of the rewards and merchandise that we'd be offering. The campaign would run for about forty days, considered by Daly to be an ideal time to maximize donations without becoming stale. It would begin on March 11, 2014, the same day Neil was scheduled to deliver a keynote address at South by Southwest (SXSW), the annual music and entertainment conference in Austin, Texas.

Our internal goal was to raise $1.5 million, a number that seemed ambitious but was the minimum we'd need to complete the design and begin manufacturing. It was certainly not anywhere near enough to fund all of our manufacturing needs, but it was enough to keep us going while the search for serious funding continued. Following Strickler's advice, we set the goal at $800,000—low enough to reach, but half of what we thought we'd need.

We had very little time between when we decided to crowdfund, in January, and the campaign launch, in March. The plan was for Neil to meet with the press covering SXSW the day after the Kickstarter began and to provide the first demo of Pono with the latest design, assuming Hansen was able to complete his prototype in time. That would help create more awareness of the campaign and improve our chances of reaching our goal.

Hansen and his engineers were hard at work on their design in Boulder and agreed to try to have their first demo in time for this SXSW press briefing. The prototype that would be shown would look nothing like a Pono, because it was all built by hand, months away from designing the circuit board that would hopefully fit. It would be several circuit boards with a jumble of wires, switches, and components.

The rewards we'd offer to Kickstarter supporters for their donations would be Pono players, as well as signed posters, shirts, and tickets to several group dinners with Neil. Early supporters would get the best deals on the players, and others would be enticed to jump in as they saw the early offerings being gobbled up, with the remaining players going for successively higher prices.

COST AND TIME?

As part of the preparation for the Kickstarter campaign, I needed to provide a delivery date and pricing for the players offered. Ship dates are notoriously hard to predict at this stage because of the uncertainty about the problems that lie ahead. The product cost would depend on the final parts being used (called the bill of materials, or BOM), the manufacturer's costs to manage and assemble it, and their profit. All of these costs depended on how many units we would build. We were months away from knowing any of these details with much certainty.

I had to come up with numbers to use; a date and price that would be attractive enough for supporters, but not so far-out or expensive that the campaign might fail. After considerable head-scratching, I estimated that we'd be able to start delivering the product in about seven months, in October. I estimated the cost, based on the parts we used for the first design, and assumed the new design would not add very much more. The other uncertainties were the manufacturer's assembly cost and margin and the volume we'd build. I decided to use an estimate of $175 as our cost for the player. That was based on about $140 in material costs at the time and a belief we could make inroads in that cost with higher volumes. That turned out to be fairly accurate.

To be able to offer a variety of Pono models on Kickstarter with different prices to entice early pledges, we offered the player in two colors, yellow and black, with the first 100 units of each color being sold for $199, and successive units at $299, compared to a suggested retail price of $399. The $399 was determined by what we considered the maximum selling price should be. While that limited our margin if the cost was really $175, I was confident the cost would be lower as the volume grew, but that anything greater than $399 retail would seriously restrict sales. We all thought $299 was a much more attractive retail price but decided to settle on $399. Even that price would make it difficult to sell at retail and still provide much profitability.

ARTISTS' EDITIONS

Shortly before the Kickstarter campaign was to begin, Neil called me and asked if we could make some special artists' editions of the players in chrome in addition to the yellow and black ones. Neil and Elliot had been talking with other artists and their managers, asking for their participation in the campaign, since Pono was, in fact, an artists' movement and many of them were early investors. Elliot told me that we got the go-ahead to create limited-edition players representing thirty different artists/groups supporting Pono: Pearl Jam, Metallica, Crosby, Stills & Nash, Tom Petty, Foo Fighters, Patti Smith, James Taylor, Herbie Hancock, Red Hot Chili Peppers, Norah Jones, Beck, Willie Nelson, Dave Matthews, Arcade Fire, The Grateful Dead, The Eagles, Buffalo Springfield, Jackson Browne, Lenny Kravitz, Elton John, Mumford and Sons, My Morning Jacket, ZZ Top, Tegan

and Sara, Lyle Lovett, Emmylou Harris, Kings of Leon, Kenny Rogers, Neil Young with Crazy Horse, and Portugal. The Man.

And of course, there was a Neil Young edition.

There would be 500 serialized units for each artist with their names and signatures engraved on the players, and one of their albums preloaded, all in a special package that included a leather case. They would sell for $100 more, at $400, and they'd never be available again once the campaign was over.

The enclosures on the standard players were molded plastic with a rubberized, soft-touch paint finish. The challenge for the special-edition products was to be able to plate the plastic parts to look like metal and find a way to etch the artists' names on them.

It was another example of Neil's creative thinking to come up with new ideas, even if it was at the last minute. Of course, we can make them, I answered, wondering to myself, *Just how?* Somehow, I'd find a way. That night I emailed John Garvey, the head of engineering at our manufacturer, PCH, in China, and explained what Neil wanted. By the time I woke up the next morning, he had emailed me that it could be done, and I'd have samples a few days later. This kind of can-do response is one of the benefits of manufacturing in China. It's never a month, rarely a week, and usually a day or two to get answers. They just work on a much more compressed time scale than their US counterparts.

Franz Krachtus, a graphic designer and friend I had brought on to help, created Photoshop images of the various versions of the players for the Kickstarter site. I asked him to make images of chrome-finished limited-edition players with artists' signatures. A few hours later, he sent me the files and they looked just like the real product.

Building the Kickstarter website involved lots of work in order for us to tell the story. It used video, still images, and dialogue. Since Neil had told the story so often, the messaging would be clear: it was about saving the music and bringing music fans an easy way to buy and listen to the world's finest recordings. The highlight of the site was the video of Neil demoing the player to dozens of his artist and music executive friends riding in his car and experiencing their reactions in real time.

The Kickstarter site went live at noon Austin time on March 15, four hours before Neil began his keynote speech. Neil posted this message to his artist friends:

> *First, we say thanks to all of you artists who have been here with Pono since the beginning. We are deeply grateful for your encouragement and support.*
>
> *When you and your recording team go into a studio or recording environment to create your latest music, there are many choices for you to make. Besides the studios, songs, players, singers, producers, engineers, microphones, and other equipment, you have the ability to choose from the numerous digital resolutions at your disposal to capture your sound. This is where Pono can make a giant difference.*
>
> *You no longer have to be satisfied with MP3 or CD being what your fans hear. Pono plays back anything you can create, just as you made it, in the digital domain.*
>
> *If you are an artist who has been recording for years and this has been your life and always will be, your original creations in analog can be transferred to the highest quality digital*

and heard anew with Pono. No longer do your original record-ings have to be the compressed sound of CDs and MP3s.

If you are a new artist, always released on MP3s and CDs, then your horizon has just been radically expanded. You can now record in whatever resolution you choose, and your fans will hear the same quality you heard in the studio. You no lon-ger have to lose part of your sound when it goes to the people. You are no longer limited by a format. Now your audience can hear what you hear.

The Pono music player can bring new light to all of your creations through Pono Music.

Record companies, this is an opportunity to rescue the art of recorded sound. Why should a Frank Sinatra recording or an Adele recording or a Nirvana, Rolling Stones, Beatles, Led Zeppelin, Who, or classical recording be limited to the CD for-mat for the future? This music is world cultural history. All of this cultural history should be preserved for enjoyment of the people in its highest possible form forever. In the twenty-first century, people, and art, deserve this technology. Bring it on. Now, as never before, it is possible.

Our listeners should hear what we heard.

Thanks for listening,
Neil Young

This message was posted on Kickstarter to potential donors:

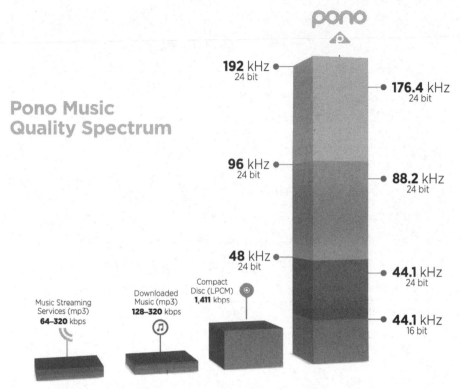

Pono Music
Quality Spectrum

192 kHz
24 bit

176.4 kHz
24 bit

96 kHz
24 bit

88.2 kHz
24 bit

48 kHz
24 bit

44.1 kHz
24 bit

44.1 kHz
16 bit

Compact
Disc (LPCM)
1,411 kbps

Downloaded
Music (mp3)
128–320 kbps

Music Streaming
Services (mp3)
64–320 kbps

How Pono quality was explained on Kickstarter

What is Pono Music?

"Pono" is Hawaiian for righteous. What righteous means to our founder Neil Young is honoring the artist's intention and the soul of music. That's why he's been on a quest, for a few years now, to revive the magic that has been squeezed out of digital music. In the process of making music more convenient—easier to download and more portable—we have sacrificed the emotional impact that only higher quality music

can deliver. However, the world has changed in the last ten years—technology has solved some of the underlying problems that forced that tradeoff. You no longer have to choose between quality and convenience when listening to music—you can have both. This is the fundamental idea behind Pono Music.

Pono's mission is to provide the best possible listening experience of your favorite music.

We are pursuing this vision by building a system for the entire music listening experience—from the original master recordings to the PonoMusic.com store to the portable Pono Player. So now you'll hear the nuances, the soft touches, and the ends on the echo—the texture and the emotion of the music the artist worked so hard to create.

Thanks for listening,
Neil Young

KICKSTARTER KICKOFF

Once the Kickstarter campaign began, it didn't take long to go from worrying if we'd ever hit $800,000 to being overwhelmed with excitement and enthusiasm. From pessimism to optimism, from planning our demise to being able to accomplish our mission; all those emotions occurred over a short twenty-four-hour time span as the money poured in. By the time Neil finished his talk at SXSW at about 5 PM, just a few hours after the campaign went live, we had reached $500,000. Over dinner a few hours later at a local restaurant, I sat next to Neil, quickly graphing the totals as a function of time on a napkin. (I later learned there was an app for that.) It showed an increase of about $100,000 each hour.

Our initial hesitation that we might not hit our minimum disappeared minutes after the campaign had begun. From the response, it seemed that there really might be an untapped market for high-quality music. At least that was what we believed at the time.

Our excitement and giddiness were suddenly interrupted the next morning with a surprise. Bob Stuart contacted our lawyer, Rick Cohen, and said we were disclosing confidential information on our Kickstarter website. He was referring to an image of the inside of the Pono player that showed the prototype circuit board, including the programmable memory chip that was to store his software—the software that hadn't arrived.

I thought his complaint was unfounded because there was nothing that was proprietary in the image that would indicate anything related to his technology, and nothing that he designed. In fact, his backing out of our arrangement required us to design around the chip in order to get our early prototypes to work. The chips simply just sat on the boards unused.

But Cohen requested that we remove the images from our Kickstarter website right away. I called Franz and he quickly edited out the chip from the image.

To my astonishment, Cohen then asked that I recall all fifty prototypes that were in the hands of our employees, board members, and beta testers and destroy them! These prototypes cost us many thousands of dollars and were needed for testing and development work. That made no sense to me and I explained that it would seriously affect our ability to continue development and testing. I called Neil and Elliot, who advised me to follow Cohen's advice, but agreed to allow Dave Gallatin and Dave Paulsen to hold on to their players and keep working on the design. (Cohen declined an interview for this book.)

Stuart's call cast a momentary pall over the campaign, with all of us fearful that he might try to interfere with it, perhaps even try to shut it down. Some of us surmised that Stuart might have been upset that we were using audio technology from Charley Hansen and Ayre Acoustics, a competitor. This was all so ironic, since Stuart still owned a sizable chunk of Pono. Fortunately, that was the last we heard from him about our Kickstarter campaign.

Money continued to pour in. First, we hoped to hit $2 million, then $3 million. At the end of the campaign, 18,220 individuals contributed, including 17,159 who pledged $200 to $400 for the music players. We raised a total of $6.2 million—at the time, Kickstarter's second-highest-grossing hardware campaign and third largest among all categories.

Rolling Stone magazine described the results:

The campaign closed out at over $6 million on April 15th with full backing on several pledges tied to rewards, including signature series Ponos bearing pre-loaded music and autograph inscriptions by Metallica, Tom Petty, Pearl Jam and, of course, Young. Two of the rewards for the top-priced $5,000 pledge levels—dinner and VIP listening parties with Young in California and New York City—also sold out. In total, 18,220 people backed the campaign, pledging $6,225,354. Kickstarter's rules *say that project organizers can keep money raised above and beyond the initial funding threshold.*[7]

We were all elated. We proved there was interest, and we had the funding to finish developing the music store and player and begin manufacturing.

KICKSTARTER PLAYER BACKERS BY COUNTRY

Country	No. of Backers
United States	8,582
Canada	1,312
United Kingdom	1,054
Australia	685
Germany	622
Japan	617
Netherlands	343
France	317
Switzerland	249
Sweden	193
Italy	180
Norway	173
Spain	161
Belgium	150
New Zealand	133

7   Kory Grow, "Neil Young's Pono Kickstarter Raises Over $6 Million," *Rolling Stone*, April 15, 2014, https://www.rollingstone.com/music/music-news/neil-youngs-pono -kickstarter-raises-over-6-million-189401/.

Country	No. of Backers
Denmark	122
Singapore	94
Hong Kong	81
Ireland	80
Brazil	75
Austria	63
Czech Republic	62
Mexico	61
Finland	58
Israel	46
Russian Federation	33
Taiwan	27
China	24
Chile	20
United Arab Emirates	20
South Africa	20
Portugal	19
Malaysia	18
Thailand	16
Poland	16
India	15
Greece	11
Luxembourg	11
Korea, Republic of	11
Hungary	9
Indonesia	8
Iceland	4

Country	No. of Backers
Brunei Darussalam	4
Philippines	4
Peru	4
Latvia	4
Jersey	3
Turkey	3
Malta	3
Slovenia	3
Croatia	3
Belarus	3
Ukraine	3
Lithuania	2
Cyprus	2
Cayman Islands	2
Macao	2
Argentina	2
Oman	2
Bulgaria	2
Qatar	2
Bermuda	2
Romania	2
Vietnam	2
Bahrain	2
Estonia	2
Maldives	1
Costa Rica	1
New Caledonia	1

Country	No. of Backers
Pakistan	1
Uruguay	1
Mauritius	1
Guadeloupe	1
Greenland	1
Colombia	1
French Polynesia	1
Saudi Arabia	1
Kuwait	1
Azerbaijan	1
Moldova, Republic of	1
Lebanon	1
Grand Total	**15,876**

Chapter 19 | Phil

THE DRIVE FROM KICKSTARTER TO PRODUCTION

The success of the Kickstarter campaign provided us all with a huge boost in confidence and morale. It brought us some stability and the ability to function beyond week to week. While not giving us enough money to complete everything we needed to do, we thought it would now be easier to bring in outside funding. Most importantly, it gave the company and its products some respect. Pono was now taken more seriously by our development partners, the public, and the press. We felt that there really was a community that cared about music quality, validated by the sizable number of people willing to vote with their pocketbooks. Neil's message had

resonated far and wide. Articles appeared about Pono's success in a wide range of magazines, blogs, and online publications from around the world in dozens of languages. There was excitement, optimism, and a new urgency to complete the development of the player and music store.

KICKSTARTER DOLLARS

As beneficial as the Kickstarter funds were, they carried with it a number of obligations. "Raised $6.2 million" is not an accurate description. Yes, we received $5.6 million after Kickstarter and Amazon took their fees, but with the money came the obligation to deliver more than 15,000 players by a given date.

We estimated that our cost of manufacturing of the players and the shipping fees to be about $3 million, roughly $200 per player. That left $2.6 million to be used to finish the development, go into production, and begin to market it. I referred to the proceeds as "Kickstarter dollars." In our case, 6.2 million Kickstarter dollars equated to 2.6 million real dollars remaining to be used for everything else—still a substantial sum that would allow us to move forward with thousands of enthusiastic supporters encouraging our efforts.

KICKSTARTER AND DEVELOPMENT

Kickstarter has radically altered the product development process. Normally, a product is announced only after its design is done, with samples built, tested, and close to being shipped. The product might even go through some changes, based on market testing and feedback from early testers.

The product comes to market when it's ready, not on a pre-determined date set months in advance. The cost is determined when the design is close to completion, the manufacturer has had a chance to build a few hundred units, and the manufacturing pricing agreements are negotiated and agreed to. There's just no way to accurately estimate the cost of a new product six months before it's completed.

Kickstarter's crowdfunding flips this on its head. Its rules require that the product cost and delivery date be committed much earlier, before they're known. Kickstarter's rules encourage optimism and aggressive pricing. Once made, you can't go back.

In addition, everything is being done under the scrutiny of the backers. While they have no insight into day-to-day issues, you can feel their presence and try to respond to their requests for frequent updates. While mostly very supportive, some in the community can be demanding and sometimes even hostile; a few expect to know every detail of progress and can easily arouse the suspicions of others.

Wariness on their part is understandable, because products introduced on Kickstarter generally have a poor record of being completed on time or even at all. Many campaigns overpromise because the companies have limited experience in delivering a product. On the positive side, we now had thousands of backers who had demonstrated their interest in high res, believed in our vision, and would become a community of supporters—all assuming we met our commitments and their expectations.

We were not overly concerned about being able to deliver the players. Our team was experienced and had developed scores of products, and we thought we were realistic about our timetable. But there still were many uncertainties about whether we could do everything we said we could, in the time we said and at the cost we committed.

In retrospect, offering the product for $300 was probably a mistake. It gave us too little margin to effectively sell at retail and barely enough profit to pay for all of the development, particularly for the escalating costs of building the music store, which always seemed to be higher than estimated. We chose a price low enough to make the campaign successful but not high enough to give us all the funds that we would need. Clearly, we'd have been much better off pricing the players higher, even if it meant selling fewer.

Our immediate goal was now to accelerate the development process to incorporate Hansen's new design, build more prototypes, and prepare for manufacturing. Before the Kickstarter success, it was hard to take manufacturing seriously. It now became critical, with the commitment to deliver more than 15,000 units just six months away.

Chapter 15 | Phil

GOING TO CHINA

There was never any question that we'd need to build the Pono player in China to meet our schedule and cost targets. While we would have preferred to manufacture the players in the United States, it just wasn't practical. The US is not competitive for building products like this because most of the components that go into it are made in China, such as the touch display, battery, and electronics. If we built the product in the US, we'd need to ship the parts well in advance, adding considerable costs and delays. When I examined the option at Neil's request, I found that the player would cost more than double if it were made in the US. Most importantly, manufacturing it in China would allow us to do it much more quickly, using existing companies with lots of experience in building consumer electronic products, an area sorely lacking in the US.

LIAM CASEY

Shortly after beginning the player development with Neil, I introduced him to Liam Casey, the CEO of PCH China Solutions. I had worked with Casey and PCH on previous projects, and his company had experience in many areas of manufacturing, including building accessories for Apple, as well as a number of more complex products. He had a capable staff of manufacturing engineers, project managers, packaging designers, buyers, and other support personnel headquartered in Shenzhen, the heart of China's consumer electronics industry.

PCH's primary expertise was in logistics: packaging, shipping, and sourcing products and parts throughout China; doing some manufacturing; and providing direct delivery of products to customers all over the world. The company had gained its experience by working on accessories for Apple, Amazon, Barnes & Noble, Beats, Fujitsu, and other consumer electronic companies.

The demands of these companies, particularly Apple, had given PCH the skills to work on products that were of the highest quality, beautifully finished, and with an excellent out-of-box experience.

While we could have reached out to other companies and conducted a manufacturing search, we had little time, few resources, and no significant financial history, which some companies required.

Another concern was product cost. Since the product was still being designed, any manufacturing agreement at this stage would be based not on a fixed price, but on a formula based on what the cost of the components (the BOM) turned out to be. Typically, based on the many electronic consumer products I've built in China, the cost of manufacturer charges equals the cost of the BOM multiplied by a factor ranging from 1.2 to 1.5, which accounts for the manufacturer's cost of labor, overhead, and profit. The exact numbers are negotiated once the design is close to completion, when you have a better sense of the design, manufacturing challenges, and the volume.

Casey was an energetic, creative, and charismatic leader with some of the best sales skills I ever saw. He had a charming Irish accent and a can-do attitude that was contagious; people loved being around him. He was constantly traveling between the US, Europe, and Asia, spending much of his time in his modern Shenzhen offices. Behind his smooth facade was a smart, thoughtful visionary who was always looking to take on the next challenge. He had built skilled, capable organizations in Shenzhen, San Francisco, and Ireland, and was focused on servicing companies developing consumer electronic products. He loved working with startups and had founded one of the first hardware incubators in San Francisco, Highway1, where he helped entrepreneurs turn their ideas into products.

PCH had grown to almost a billion dollars in sales, but most of its business was low-margin work for Apple, much of it logistics and light assembly. He had been trying to diversify beyond Apple by taking on another large customer, the headphone company Beats. But once Apple bought Beats, he was back to having mostly one large and difficult customer.

So, our timing was good. Casey had been wanting to take on more challenging projects, such as playing a larger role in a product's development by becoming involved earlier in the process.

Casey wanted to build Pono in his own factory, even though it was more complex than the accessories he normally built. He liked

Liam Casey, CEO of PCH,
our manufacturer

the high visibility of the product and the desire to support Neil's efforts, and it was a way to expand his company's expertise.

PCH proposed setting up a new production line especially for Pono. I worried that doing Pono was a larger and more complex project than he had typically done, and this might be a stretch. But with limited time, and few other options, I thought that PCH could do it. Unlike other companies, if we ran into a problem, I had the CEO's phone number—actually three numbers, for each of the three iPhones he carried.

TIME OF GREAT INTENSITY

The next six months from the completion of the Kickstarter campaign to the manufacturing of Pono players was the most intense, pressure-packed, self-reflecting period of time I've ever spent developing a product, a result of the tight time pressure and high visibility. Yet, there was no direct pressure from Neil, Elliot, or John. They just assumed I knew what I was doing, and that it would get done. That added even more pressure.

On many of my product development projects there had been a larger team, with my role primarily being to direct their efforts. But this project was different. We had a tiny hardware team with a very limited budget. So, I decided that I needed to be much more hands on, involved in the product at a much deeper level than I had been for a long time. I felt the responsibility and commitment to Neil to get this right. And we needed somebody to pay attention to every detail while still not micromanaging the team. Experience had taught me that, with startups, one detail could kill or seriously hobble a new product as well as the company itself. You can't afford recalls or do-overs. You get one chance to get it right.

While Pono was a relatively straightforward, even predictable design effort, as with any product, there are always a myriad of issues that arise, many impossible to predict. If you're too optimistic, you might miss a potential issue that could seriously impact the product, and if you're too pessimistic, you end up worrying about many things that never happen. I was the pessimist this time and would worry about all the things that *could* go wrong. With such a small team and with my being in charge, I felt it was incumbent on me to do so.

WORRY LIST

Writing down my concerns had been useful when developing other products, and was therapeutic as well, so that was where I began. I created my "Worry List." It contained potential issues that would keep me awake at night—high-risk items that could jeopardize the product's performance, quality, schedule, and ultimately its success. The list was easy to compile, having done so for many products and experiencing almost every kind of problem over the years.

Top on my list was audio quality. We were packing hundreds of tiny components from Hansen's new design into the small player. So many things could go wrong, even if his design worked. Would everything fit? Would the audio be noticeably better, and would his design even be manufacturable? How would we test the audio quality, and how consistent would it be across all units? When I asked Hansen about these worries, even he didn't know for sure. He was honest, which was his charm. "I've never done anything quite like this before in a high-volume portable product," he said, "but I sure hope it all works."

One of my other big concerns was the Pono's touch display. Creating a custom color touch display from scratch was too expensive and would have required committing to buy a very large volume—perhaps 100,000 pieces—to get a willing supplier. Instead we selected an off-the-shelf two-inch color display with a touch panel that was being used in pocket-size cameras. We found just one company with this size of display that was willing to work with us. And while the display was fairly standard, we still would need some customization to make it fit.

I was also worried about battery life, how long it would last between charges. Hansen's design would consume more power than the amplifier chips they replaced. We had chosen the largest possible battery that would fit, but until we built prototypes using the actual circuitry and fine-tuned the firmware, battery life was difficult to predict. We hoped for ten hours of play, but early calculations predicted only three. We eventually were able to get to seven hours. Had the life been much shorter, we might have had to consider redoing the entire mechanical design to accommodate a larger battery.

We debated how much memory to build into the player. Because high-resolution files use more memory, what would be enough? Would customers still expect to carry thousands of albums in their pocket? We selected a 64GB memory chip to be built into the player and provided a memory slot for adding additional memory. At the time, 64GB was the sweet spot for the cost-versus-memory curve, as it offered the most memory per dollar. We were so concerned about the customer's need to store many albums at once that we included an additional 64GB memory card with the player at the outset, so that customers would have 128GB, enough for eighty to a hundred high-res albums. That added $30 to the player's cost. We later surveyed customers and found that few cared about player memory, because they could keep their files on their computer and easily load what they wanted to hear, so we eventually eliminated the extra memory card. It was not lost on those of us who had agonized over losing Stuart's memory-saving software that it wasn't that big of an issue, after all.

MORE HELP

As I took on more of the development and manufacturing of Pono, I realized I needed an additional engineer to focus all of their time on quality and manufacturing. We needed to deliver products that worked well and were free of defects. We couldn't afford to suffer from early failures. It would be embarrassing for the player to fail, even worse than not shipping on time. I wanted an engineer familiar with quality, testing, and manufacturing, one who would be willing to spend lots of time in China immersed in all of these issues with PCH and the part suppliers.

I searched for candidates using LinkedIn and found Greg Chao, an engineer from Silicon Valley with lots of experience in product quality and manufacturing and who had worked on many hardware products being made in China.

MORE PROBLEMS

As expected, we encountered a variety of problems over the next few months as we went from building prototypes to beginning production. We seemed always to be scrambling to find parts. Lead times for electrical components were often several months, but we needed them in weeks, so we had to find them on the secondary market at elevated prices. Sometimes PCH or their supplier forgot to place an order for parts, and we had to scramble. Not having a specific part, even one that cost less than a penny, would halt production.

A few supplier problems occurred that caused us to debate whether we should change to another supplier and start over. The company that assembled the electronic circuit board had difficulty building it because of inexperience with assembling the memory onto the processor. We debated whether to wait and see if they could solve their problems or find someone new. To make things more difficult, every company in China tells you "no problem," so it's hard to know the true facts. We stuck with them and they eventually figured it out.

One morning after arriving on one of my frequent trips to China, I asked PCH to take me to the battery fabricator that they had selected based on a referral. A fabricator buys the power cells from the battery manufacturer, in this case Samsung, and adds a custom protection circuit and connector. After arriving at their offices, we were aghast at what we saw: a dirty and disorganized factory with sloppy assembly practices. We quickly switched suppliers, perhaps avoiding a calamity down the road.

These experiences led me to bring in an old friend for several months, Reynold Starnes, a retired engineering VP who had headed up Hewlett-Packard's desktop computer group, to evaluate the suppliers and work with PCH to procure parts. Starnes was an expert on Asian manufacturing and would work with his counterparts at PCH.

TOUCH DISPLAY

Meanwhile, the touch display was giving us problems during prototype testing. Our software quality engineer, Damani Jackson, noticed during his testing that the displays on some Pono players would react on their own, as if someone had touched the display. It was random and hard to reproduce, but it occurred often enough to worry us. The effect was that a song that was playing would stop or another would start playing on its own. We called it "false touch." Every problem gets a name!

Dave Gallatin spent several weeks digging into this, and after much sleuthing, discovered the cause—spurious electronic signals between the two circuits controlling the display and the touch screen. We informed PCH and Greg Chao flew to China to meet with them and the display company. After they did their own investigation and were able to duplicate the problem, the display supplier said that the only fix was for them to redesign the circuitry in the touch display to eliminate the electrical interference, a process they estimated would take about four months. That was a shock and one we just couldn't accept. It would be a huge blow to meeting our promised delivery date.

After discovering the cause, we were able to induce failures on about half the players. Gallatin kept working on the problem and thought he might be able to come up with a solution. Ten days later, he had developed a clever but very complex fix that would use firmware to automatically have each player analyze the characteristics of its display and then make an adjustment to reduce the likelihood of a false touch—essentially have each Pono test and repair itself.

It took another month to design, test, and implement, but we were uncertain whether this fix would work well enough on all of the players to be able to ship the product. Would it reduce the 50 percent failure rate to 10 percent or 5 percent? We really wouldn't know until we began production and were able to build and test hundreds of players.

Until that could happen, all of us in the company worried about this on a daily basis. PCH added a test to the assembly line where they'd try to induce false touch on every player for twenty minutes at an elevated temperature, where the problem had occurred more frequently. We eventually reduced the occurrence on production units to close to zero, and it was never an issue once we shipped the players.

Testing for false touch

What we went through with Pono, dealing with a myriad of problems and surprises, was no different from what most products with any complexity experience. Every product has issues, many unanticipated and not discovered until hundreds or thousands of them are built.

While all of this was going on with the music player, another team was hard at work on the other big requirement of Pono, a method by which customers could browse, purchase, and download music into the player: the Pono music store.

Chapter 16 | Phil

BUILDING THE PONO MUSIC STORE

P edram Abrari had a very difficult job and little time to do it: quickly build the Pono music store and all the related software. The site would need to be able to easily scale to handle our expected large number of customers from around the world. It was a huge task that needed to be completed by the time the players were shipped in October.

A SIMPLE EXPERIENCE

Neil's vision was for the store to be much simpler to use than the existing sites that sold downloaded music files, and he wanted it to be focused on high-res music. He wanted to show only one album of any performance, the one with the highest-quality audio—not the multiple versions of the same album at different quality levels sold on other stores. Neil's promise was, "If you bought it from Pono, you could be assured it was the best available."

Neil also wanted every album's resolution level to be clearly labeled and searchable. He also wanted to add much more high-res content by going directly to the artists, their managers, and the record companies, searching their archives and remastering existing masters. The goal was to offer much more high-res content than any other store.

PONO PROMISE

Neil and Franz Krachtus created the look and feel of the store's design, and Neil provided several other innovative ideas. One of the most unique was "The Pono Promise." This was a feature that encouraged customers not to delay their purchase of an album that might not currently be available in high resolution—more likely just at CD quality. If the customer purchased an album that later became available at a higher resolution, they'd be given the upgraded album at no cost.

This was a revolutionary idea and reflected Neil's concern and respect for his fans. He was adamant that Pono users should not need to pay for the same performance a second time. We'd also use our relationship with our customers to report back to the record companies to let them know which recordings our customers wanted most in high res.

While we wanted the record labels to pick up this cost, they turned us down, so Pono paid for it. Neil was passionate about this issue, because buying the same performance time after time has been a part of the record labels' operating model, which Neil knew really upset customers and reflected poorly on the artists. Music fans have been asked to purchase the same album multiple times with no consideration for past purchases. They bought it on vinyl, then on different tape formats, and finally on CD. Our store would only carry albums that were at minimum CD quality, 44.1/16, nothing lower. While that's at the very low end of passable quality and not high res, sadly it's the only format available for many albums.

DEVELOPING THE STORE

Developing the Pono music store was essentially creating iTunes for the Pono player in just six months. It was incredibly difficult and expensive to do and would end up costing millions of dollars. Pedram would need to identify partners who could meet our needs for the various aspects of the ecosystem, establish partnerships with each of them, and then manage all their activities with our internal team to create a state-of-the-art, seamless experience.

There were five main components that we needed: (1) the storefront, (2) the management of the music files and metadata (the information about each of the music files that accompany an album), (3) a payment processing service, (4) the desktop software used to manage our customers' music library and to load their music onto the Pono player, and (5) the Pono player software. This would work like an app and include the user interface; the player settings, adjustments, and controls; and the music management.

Of these components, the only one that we would build from scratch was the Pono player software. If we were to deliver the rest on time, we had to rely on partners with expertise and existing products in each of the areas.

USING SALESFORCE TO POWER THE MUSIC STORE

Pedram started his research into the e-commerce platforms available to build the storefront. Unlike most online stores, which carry hundreds or thousands of products for sale, online music stores offer millions, and most e-commerce platforms can't handle this well. After an exhaustive search, Pedram realized that none of the available platforms could meet our needs, and he'd need to find another solution.

Meanwhile, the Kickstarter community discussion board continued to remain active long after the Kickstarter campaign ended, and it became a hangout for music fans, where there were vibrant discussions about Pono, new music, and audio quality. That gave Pedram an idea of bringing this level of discussion into the music store, where customers could continue to interact with one another. He thought of using Salesforce, a popular cloud-based software development platform used to manage a business's relationship with its customers, including customer support, a user community, and direct marketing. At their 2013 Dreamforce conference, he had seen their new Community Cloud product, which let companies connect to their customers to share information.

Pedram thought, *Why not use Salesforce's platform, Force.com, to build the music store?*

But there was one big problem. Salesforce was a business-to-business platform, not the business-to-consumer platform that was required. This meant Pedram would need to build an online store from scratch or find someone who had already done it. He found a small company in Chicago, CloudCraze, that had such a platform and also aspired to integrate it with Community Cloud to deliver the experience he had envisioned. Pedram emailed Cloud-Craze's CEO, Bill Loumpouidis, and heard back the next day. Bill was a die-hard Neil Young fan and jumped at the opportunity to build the user interface for buying music, checkout, and payment.

When Pedram proposed the idea of building a social music store on Salesforce to Neil and the Pono board at the next board meeting, it was well received, especially because of Marc Benioff, founder and CEO of Salesforce, who was a great friend of Neil's.

While small companies such as ours cannot usually afford to use the Salesforce platform, Marc changed the Salesforce pricing model to accommodate Pono's needs.

This partnership effectively turned Salesforce into a business-to-consumer platform, and Pedram believed it may have planted the seeds that eventually resulted in the Salesforce business-to-consumer services available today.

MANAGING THE MUSIC

Now that the social music-store technology had been found, the next step was to solve the challenge of storing, delivering, and managing the music content. There were really only a few companies who had experience with storing high-res music and had the licenses from the recording companies to do so. The leader in the space was Omnifone, a cloud-based music consumption service based in London. Pedram reached out to them and, once again, Neil's name opened doors. Within a couple of weeks, we had an agreement for Omnifone to ingest all the high-res content available to Pono from the three major music labels, using software that connected to our music store and desktop applications.

Pono's engineers worked with Omnifone for months to bring in the content, quality-check the music, tag the files with the resolution of the albums, and feed all this information into the Pono music store. In this process, we identified and solved numerous problems and inefficiencies in the whole end-to-end process with the music labels, benefitting all of Omnifone's customers at the same time.

THE DESKTOP APPS

The last element we needed was the desktop software to deliver an iTunes-like experience. It would allow Pono users to download their purchased music, manage their music library, and load their music onto the Pono player.

Pedram contacted JRiver, a company that had built a desktop software app for Windows that was similar to iTunes but more complex because of its numerous features for technologists and audiophiles. JRiver's CEO, Jim Hillegass, was also a Neil Young fan but was very skeptical of Pono and our odds of success. Nevertheless, he agreed to work with us to deliver a Pono-branded version of their desktop software for both Windows and Mac computers.

Altogether, building the store was a huge undertaking that involved close coordination between Pono, Salesforce, Cloud-Craze, Omnifone, and JRiver, as well as the record labels, while dealing with the inevitable technical issues that occurred with their integration.

I was skeptical that we'd be able to complete the store by the time we shipped the players. It was not that I doubted Pedram's abilities—he was one of the smartest people I've worked with in this area. I just thought the magnitude and complexity of the work involving five different companies, all working in parallel, was filled with risks and obstacles.

Yet Pedram, the rest of the Pono engineering team, and these partners delivered just in time. We launched the Pono music store in beta in October 2014 at Salesforce's Dreamforce event with all of the essential features. The following January, we released the 1.0 version at CES.

Chapter 17 | Phil

MORE MANAGEMENT TURMOIL

While I was working on the player and Pedram was working on the Pono music store, a drama was simultaneously unfolding among some of the company's management that I had little knowledge of at the time. John Hamm realized that the company needed to raise more funding and had been searching for investors ever since he arrived. After the successful Kickstarter campaign, he increased his efforts and was slowly making progress.

FINDING AN INVESTOR

Spending was steadily increasing to build the music store and all it entailed, and to prepare for manufacturing the player. But we had no budget for marketing, nor plans beyond fulfilling the Kickstarter orders. John met with potential investors who might be willing to make a substantial investment, perhaps three or four million dollars. After several months of effort, he brought in a private investor who agreed to invest four million dollars. One of the conditions of the investment would be that the composition of the board of directors be changed to reflect the new ownership.

The board had the same makeup as in the beginning, still without any members with experience running a technology startup. Hamm and the new investor made their proposal to the board for the investment and a corresponding board change, explaining that such a change was normal and customary to reflect the new ownership.

Hamm also requested that Rick Cohen, who was still serving as a personal lawyer to several of the board members as well as to the company, would need to choose one or the other role, since it would be a conflict of interest to do both.

Behind closed doors, according to Neil and Elliot, Cohen painted a negative picture of the investment offer to the board and told them that Hamm was likely trying to take control of the company and was intentionally removing those board members closest to Neil.

The confrontation escalated quickly, and some on the board thought that Hamm presented the investment and board changes as a take-it-or-leave-it offer. Hamm later told me that he suggested to the board that they get another legal opinion to understand that these changes to the board were just good governance. However, neither Neil nor Elliot recalled that suggestion.

HAMM OUT

The outcome was that the board decided to request Hamm's resignation and replace him with Rick Cohen, the company's attorney, as CEO. Unlike Hamm, who had built many companies from scratch, and advised and invested in others, Cohen had much less experience in this area. Although he managed his law firm, he would now be leading a company, which required a completely different set of skills.

In my subsequent discussions with Neil and Elliot, both agreed that they made a serious error in supporting this change. Elliot, in retrospect, thought Cohen had overplayed the issue and that he and Neil were both overly influenced by him. Elliot explained, "Both Neil and I were out of our element."

They said that they had a lot of respect for Hamm and should not have terminated him; instead, they should have just turned down the investment offer. Elliot said that's what he had intended to do, rather than look for duplicity and side-dealing, and was not convinced of the accusations that Hamm was taking over the company. His only fear was that Neil would have much less power and influence, and, ultimately, Elliot believed he had to do what he thought was best for Neil.

Neil is also very loyal to the people that he works with. In this case, his loyalty extended to his board members, many of whom were his friends and had been investors from the start. Neil also had some concern about bringing on new people who might not share his vision.

These management changes further impacted the viability of the company, as it was one of the only opportunities that we ever had to bring in a sizable investment and to have the company run by an experienced CEO.

Hamm had been a no-nonsense, fast-moving CEO, sometimes a little brash and cocky, but very smart and experienced. He was always thinking ahead and thinking big, and his use for the investment was to staff up marketing and sales, begin a second-generation product, and try to purchase one of the new streaming services, leveraging some additional investors. As I saw it, his failing was that he didn't effectively convey his plans to the board, explain them, and develop support beforehand. He had found the board to be less experienced than those he had worked with and his patience had worn thin.

From the board's position, Hamm was asking for some of them to step down without adequately explaining the context and without the board having a full understanding of Hamm's long-term vision for the company. Neil now believes that losing Hamm was a pivotal moment for the company and regrets what happened.

The change of CEOs could not have occurred at a worse time. Cohen had become CEO during the fall of 2014 at the time we were preparing for production and delivery of the player and the launch of the music store, and a few months before we'd attend CES in January for our official introduction.

Chapter 18 | Phil

PREPARING FOR MASS PRODUCTION

*N*eil took intense interest in all aspects of the Pono player, particularly everything that affected sound quality, user experience, and product innovation. An example of his literally thinking *out of the box* occurred when Neil called me to discuss the sample packaging that Franz and PCH had designed. It was a black rectangular cardboard box, similar in design to what was being used for the iPhone. Neil wasn't satisfied and thought we could do much better.

A cardboard box, he explained, would be discarded by the customer, turning it into waste. Instead, he asked if we could develop a bamboo box that would be more likely to be retained and reused and not thrown away. My first thought was that it would probably be much more expensive. I had never worked with bamboo and had never seen it used this way, but the concept was intriguing.

Neil's first concept sketch for a bamboo box

It could provide a great out-of-box experience; it spoke to Neil's love of the environment and authenticity, and it could be iconic to Pono.

Neil developed some design concepts that we reviewed with PCH, who had a lot of experience in creating innovative packaging. Matthieu Charlier, their packaging head, turned Neil's sketches into several designs in just a few days. Greg Chao then visited several suppliers located near the bamboo forests in China. This was the first time, the suppliers told us, that a company wanted to use bamboo to package a consumer electronics product. The resulting design, after weeks of work and many prototypes, was elegant: a sliding lid with compartments to cradle the player and store all its accessories. The Pono logo was burned onto the cover with a laser, and the result was one of the most unique, functional, and attractive packages ever created for an electronic product. Surprisingly, it ended up costing a lot less than we expected, about

five dollars, just two dollars more than the cardboard alternative. We created two sizes, one for the yellow and black Ponos and a larger one for the special edition artist models and case.

PREPARING FOR MANUFACTURING

As we got closer to production, we addressed scores of issues that arose, all quite normal for a complex hardware product. Most importantly, we were making progress on all fronts and were on schedule to begin shipment in late October, meeting our Kickstarter goal. Much would hinge on PCH's work in setting up the new assembly area in their factory, not far from where they were packaging Apple accessories, an area heavily guarded and off limits to all of us.

The PCH team was doing a fine job building out the production area. It was being led by Jennie Yang, the manufacturing team leader, and Charlie Nolan, a manufacturing expert PCH brought in as we prepared to ramp up production. Jennie would give me daily reports of progress all the way through to product shipment. The room where the Pono was to be built began to fill up with

assembly stations, conveyor belts, and totes full of parts, in preparation for trial runs. It was exciting to see all these parts arriving
and realize how real this was becoming, going from having a few
dozen prototypes to thousands of production units. It's an exhil-
arating feeling that's hard to describe but makes all the difficult
work worthwhile.

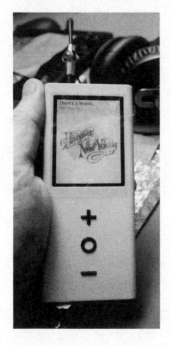

Finding all the parts we needed
to build the players continued to be a
struggle right to the moment of production. PCH and Reynold Starnes,
the former HP VP I brought in for this
purpose, had been addressing this issue
for months. It became even more challenging with the design changes Charley
Hansen made as he fine-tuned the electronics. Each change required searching for new parts and purchasing large
quantities. We were also focused on
getting the touch-screen issue resolved,
testing every unit, and then putting each
player through a sophisticated audio test that Hansen developed.
We'd have no idea of the test results until we built a few hundred
units, but in the end, the reject rate was close to zero. Hansen
had created a great design that proved easy to manufacture. In all
of our listening tests, the audio performance was spectacular, as
good as what we had hoped for and substantially better than our
original design.

FIRST SHOWING

I had strong confidence that we had a great audio design when, months earlier, I had flown to Ayre Acoustics in Boulder, Colorado, to meet with Hansen and listen to one of his first prototypes. He asked that I sit in his sound room where he operated two Pono players hidden behind my back, the original and his new design. Without identifying them, he asked me which I preferred. I was able to immediately pick the one that sounded better, which fortunately turned out to be his design.

Just prior to production, we had our first public showing of the Pono player at Salesforce's annual Dreamforce conference in San Francisco, attended by more than a hundred thousand people.

Neil and Marc Benioff at Dreamforce 2014

The Pono team at Dreamforce

Thanks to Marc Benioff, Salesforce provided a huge exhibit space for us to demo the Pono for the first time. We had soundproof listening booths where we demoed using speakers, as well as a sitting area where a dozen Pono players were set up for visitors to listen to with Sennheiser and Audeze headphones. We were overwhelmed by the crowds and the great response.

PREPARING FOR THE WORST

My concern about reliability and quality led to planning for a contingency that never happened. What do we do about defective units once the player reaches the customer? We had no idea what the failure rate might be. We tested scores of preproduction units with good results. Other than an infrequent display problem and some software bugs, the units seemed to work flawlessly. But experience had taught me that you never know what other problems might arise once you put thousands of a new product into the hands of customers. With previous hardware products, I've experienced returns from less than 1 percent to as high as 20 percent. I discussed this with Neil, and he agreed that that we should take a very conservative approach to ensure that no Kickstarter buyer would have to wait for a replacement if their unit proved to be defective. So, to be extremely cautious, we decided to build an extra 20 percent reserve.

It turned out that the number of units returned for defects was much less than expected, less than 1 percent over the entire first year—very good performance for even a mature product.

PRODUCTION BEGINS

We finally began production in early October 2014, starting slowly with a few dozen each day, increasing to nearly a thousand a day. By the third week in October, PCH had built 8,000 players. I flew to China to do a personal inspection prior to shipping any product, as one last, final check. By now I knew the product like the back of my hand, and although PCH's quality engineer, Norman Zhu,

and ours, Greg Chao, did their own tests and inspections, I had to see for myself with my own eyes. I planned to randomly select units and do everything a customer would do: push the buttons, navigate with the touch screen, play music through headphones, and inspect for cosmetic blemishes.

THE RATTLE

The day before I was to leave on my flight to Hong Kong, I got a call from Elliot's assistant, Bonnie Levetin, to tell me that one of the most recent players being tested by one of Neil's friends had been returned because it had a rattling sound inside. I asked her to ship it overnight to Dave Paulsen, so he could check it out. When I landed in Hong Kong the next day, I got a call from Paulsen saying he opened the player and found a tiny screw rattling around inside. It was one of two used to hold down the circuit board, and apparently had not been sufficiently tightened and came loose. I assumed it was simply a random occurrence and put it out of my mind.

When I went to the PCH factory the next morning, I saw 8,000 pristine players, each wrapped in glistening transparent plastic, stacked up in trays ready to be packaged in their bamboo boxes with their accessories. I randomly selected a hundred units from among the stacked trays and took them into an adjacent conference room to try each one out, accompanied by several members of the production team and PCH's project manager, Carlos Martin.

Martin, who was my key project contact at PCH along with Jennie, was a Spanish-born engineer who moved to Shenzhen to work in product development and manufacturing. He was one of PCH's best program managers, and we would speak several times a week for nearly two years. He was instrumental to making Pono happen, once we engaged with PCH.

PCH Pono project leaders:
Carlos Martin and Jennie Yang

I picked several of the players up from the table and checked their appearance. They all looked perfect.

I then recalled the unit with a rattle and was going to ask about it, but instead I just shook one of the players, much to the surprise of those who were watching. No rattle, but lots of puzzled looks. I methodically went through the entire sample of one hundred, shaking each of them, and found about a third had a rattling sound.

I still remember the expressions on everyone's faces, all with stunned looks, almost despondent. Martin was almost in tears, because he knew what this meant. Shaking a product is not a test we'd normally do, but because of that one defective unit, it alerted us to a serious problem just before we planned to package and ship thousands of players.

PCH production team

PCH manufacturing management team

The team convened in a nearby conference room to assess the situation, led by PCH's head of engineering, John Garvey. He quickly came up with a plan to sample each lot of players that were built on different days and shifts to see if there was a pattern. A few hours later, we reassembled, and Garvey tabulated the results on a whiteboard. He found that the players with rattles were all made over a span of three days on the day shift, about 3,000 out of the 8,000. He isolated the problem units to one assembly operator who didn't tighten the screws sufficiently. She was later instructed on how to do the operation correctly and the problem never reoccurred.

Instead of packaging and shipping the units the day I showed up, we had to open every one of the 3,000 players in the defective lots, rattle or not, and check for loose or untightened screws. The players were not easy to open, since they were held together with both snaps and silicone adhesive. One of the assembly-line opera-tors figured out how to split apart the cases using a special tool he made that looked like a credit card with a cylindrical handle along its edge, allowing him to slice along the seam carefully but with a strong force. I was relieved that I hadn't taken the engineer's advice earlier to use a design that permanently sealed the player shut and not be reparable.

Reworking Ponos for rattles
at PCH

Fortunately, we caught the defect in time and avoided the serious consequence of having to recall thousands of units to be repaired. I never faulted PCH, because incidents like this happen when starting up an assembly line and building a new product. All it takes is one operator to make a slipup, be inadequately trained, or not follow instructions to create a huge ripple effect. I couldn't imagine what would have happened if we hadn't caught this. The cost of returns and replacements and the embarrassment would have been devastating.

SHIPPING

The next day we all were in a much better mood. We watched the Pono players, accessories, quick-start guide, and a note from Neil being put into their bamboo boxes and then into individual shipping boxes. I followed the first unit to the shipping area where PCH printed UPS labels that enabled them to be sent directly to a customer's home anywhere in the world in three days or less for less than twenty dollars.

Shipping the first Pono player

The first player was going to a backer in Europe. But the label wouldn't print. An error came up on the screen that said invalid address. That's when we learned another issue about Kickstarter. They never validated the addresses that the supporters provided. Without a valid address, UPS wouldn't accept the package.

As it turned out, this was not an isolated incident. We had trouble delivering more than 300 of the more than 15,000 players. In the intervening six months from the start of the Kickstarter campaign to the time of shipping, many of the participants' addresses, emails, and phone numbers had changed, or their original addresses had been incomplete. It took us more than three months to track down those individuals and send them their players.

We experienced a few other surprises, as well. Units sent to Australia and Israel were stopped at customs because they don't allow bamboo products into their countries without doing their own material testing, which can take months. For those supporters we got the units back, and remailed them in a cardboard box.

Our commitment to the Kickstarter backers was to start shipping in October. Our first batch of players shipped on October 31 and we shipped most of the remaining in November and early December; the last unit went out just before Christmas. By Kickstarter standards, it was a very good performance and one we were pleased with. We had many happy customers who raved about their product after receiving it.

PONO COMMUNITY

Once the Kickstarter campaign came to an end in April 2014, we noticed that several backers had created an online forum to discuss Pono and other music-related subjects. Ian Kendrick from the UK, Kyle French from Texas, Eduard Nuijen from France, and Rich Gross from Israel, none of whom had met before, had spontaneously come together to create an unofficial Pono community.

The online forum was being used to discuss all sorts of topics that related to Pono, high-res music, Neil Young, and their favorite recordings. As Kendrick described it, it was an online version of music fans getting together at their favorite record store on a Saturday morning to talk about their favorite topics. Except this was occurring around the clock, seven days a week.

As the forum grew, it took on a life of its own and became the unofficial place to go for all things Pono. Participants were remarkably helpful to one another, as well as to us at Pono. It was often the first place we discovered a product bug or some issue that needed attention. It was an example of one of the positive aspects of the internet that, when used correctly, brings people with like interests together to discuss what's important to them, and provides a receptive audience for their opinions. It's also a great way for a small company to get closer to their customers and have a two-way conversation that benefits both sides. After shipping a new product or launching a new site, there's nothing more valuable than for a company to get quick feedback and learn what's working and what's not. Despite all the testing, you're always surprised by what new things customers discover when the product is experienced by hundreds or thousands.

We loved what they were doing and reached out to them to ask if they were interested in having their unofficial community become part of the Pono Music website that we'd host on the Salesforce platform. Kendrick and the others quickly accepted, and it was integrated into our site.

The community grew quickly and reached more than 50,000 members from all over the world. The forum discussions expanded, taking on dozens of music-related topics. One example was a discussion about the best way to listen to Pono in its balanced mode and what cables were best to use. One member took on the task of testing cables from different manufacturers and making recommendations. We also used the forum to keep the members up to date with additions and changes underway.

Like most forums, it required quite a bit of work to moderate and keep away the trolls—those who posted to promote a political cause, exhibited bigotry, or tried to start controversies on unrelated topics. While the four moderators had day jobs, they each spent upward of twenty to thirty hours moderating each week. For them it had become a labor of love.

Chapter 19 | Phil

THE REVIEWS ARRIVE

*O*nce the players began shipping, the music, audio, and technology press began writing about Pono, and those that received players through Kickstarter posted their own reviews, primarily on Amazon. The responses from those in the music and audio communities, as well as the new owners, were full of praise. The reviews credited Neil and Pono with doing just what was promised, delivering a player that sounded better than anything else, even better than players that cost thousands of dollars more.

Many reviews were like this one from Tyll Hertsens, posted in March 2015 on Inner Fidelity, a popular review site for audio products.[8]

---

8   Tyll Hertsens, "The Pono Player and Promises Fulfilled," *Inner Fidelity*, March 26, 2015, https://www.innerfidelity.com/content/pono-player-and-promises -fulfilled#uE5TsdzyeTG1FpDh.99.

The Pono Player was a sublimely musical surprise. While the letter of Neil Young's words were, in my view, a significant overpromising of the Pono Player's performance—I don't think anything could have objectively lived up to his "on a mission to save music" zeal—I do think the Pono Player delivers superbly on the spirit of his intent. This player delivers the sonic goods way beyond its price, and to my ears is the most satisfying handheld digital file player I've yet heard.

When I compare it side-by-side in blind tests with other players I find its smooth yet resolving treble to be its stand-out characteristic. I will also say that the sonic differences I heard between players was objectively quite subtle—all the players I used sounded quite good. But in long term listening I found the subtle beauties of the Pono Player to elicit a significantly superior emotional connection to the music for me. This may very well be personal but having heard products before that are widely held by enthusiasts as musical, I've got to think the Pono Player will fall into that category.

While he faulted the Pono for its unusual shape and small screen, he concluded with:

I'll just leave you with the knowledge that I love the sound of the Pono Player. If you want a simple but excellent sounding portable player that won't break the bank the Pono Player is an outstanding choice.

Reviews from users were equally exuberant, much along the lines of this email from Michael Farrell of Toronto, Ontario, Canada:

> For me, the PonoPlayer has been a revelation. The clarity, depth, and spaciousness of hi-res music played through the PonoPlayer is the closest thing to live music that I have ever experienced. The device is light, fits well in my hand, and is easy to navigate. And through the player's balanced mode capabilities, the quality of sound and clear distinction between musical instruments is the best that I have ever heard. I am grateful for how the PonoPlayer has enriched my music listening experiences. A total quality product.

THE GOOD AND THE UGLY

The reviews from the consumer tech press, however, were more negative—some even hostile. Their criticism was less directed to the product's audio performance—few had even tried a player before writing about it—and more about the need for high-resolution music, with some reviewers questioning whether anyone could tell the difference.

One reviewer, David Pogue of Yahoo!, who bought a player on Kickstarter, had emailed me to ask some questions about the player while he was working on his review. I asked Neil to respond directly because of Pogue's influence. Pogue responded to Neil's email:

> *Thank you, Neil . . . what an honor to hear from you!*
>
> *This is most helpful. I now realize that I've been comparing Pono's high-res music with the songs from the iTunes store, which [is] a big improvement over "low-res MP3" files . . . I imagine that explains the difference in your tests and mine!*
>
> *In any case, you're absolutely right that there's no reason for the world to go on compressing files in this age of copious storage space, and I admire what Pono is doing to get the great music remastered!*
>
> *Thanks again for taking the time to help me out!*
>
> *—dp*

But then the next day, Pogue's review appeared, titled "Neil Young's PonoPlayer: The Emperor Has No Clothes," ridiculing Neil and his efforts. Pogue conducted his own listening test by asking subjects to compare music from an iPhone using Apple earbuds and a Pono player and found the results to be inconclusive. Therefore, he concluded that the Pono and, by inference, all high-resolution music, was no better than ordinary music files. The test was flawed in so many ways, from the CD music he selected to the way he conducted the test, as many of his readers pointed out.

I called Neil to discuss Pogue's review and asked about responding. Neil told me, "Don't respond. If he can't tell the difference, that's his loss, and he shouldn't buy one." But the damage was done, and Pogue's influence would be felt.

Having written a weekly technology column for a San Diego newspaper for twelve years, I found the world of tech journalism to have many excellent writers, but also many tech bloggers who serve as echo chambers, creating little original content on their own. Pogue's review was referenced on dozens of their blogs with such headlines as "A tall refreshing drink of snake oil," "The Pono Player just sucks," "It Sure Seems Like Neil Young's Pono Player Is Bullshit," and "Neil Young's pricey PonoPlayer no better than iPhone for music."

I was disappointed by the viciousness, ridicule, and even hatred for Neil and Pono that showed up in some of the reviews from the tech community. Few talked about the technology; more talked about Neil's failed efforts, sometimes with noticeable glee.

Yet the reviews from the audio community, from those who are critical listeners of music, continued to heap accolades on the Pono and its music store. John Atkinson, editor of the highly regarded *Stereophile* magazine, praised the product and named it Digital Component of the Year:

> *Considered on its own merits, the Pono Player is a well-engineered, high-performance, portable player that is equally at home in a conventional high-end audio system, and is offered at a fair, affordable price. In combination with the Pono Music World app, it offers a plug 'n' play gateway to high-quality music reproduction.*

Neil wrote back to Atkinson and his readers:

Editor:

Hello to all Stereophile *readers. I'd like to personally thank John Atkinson and the* Stereophile *crew for your apprecia-tion of the PonoPlayer and what it delivers. I first realized that Pono had to happen when it became clear to me that we had lost the connection with music with the dominance of MP3, downloading, and streaming. The goal for Pono was sim-ple: bring the music back, for all of us. Realizing it, making it happen, was a bit more tricky. As the community around Pono has grown—currently approaching 43,000 people—we have learned more and more about how music is at the heart of what it means to be human. Latest ideas show that music prob-ably came before language, which in turn led to our culture. In many ways it is what being human is all about. We have a primordial need to make, receive, and share music. Without it we are incomplete.*

For me the ability of early digital music systems to make music was not satisfactory and so they could not satisfy that basic need we have for music. They just weren't good enough. They made sound, but not music that touches our soul like it should . . .

Many other musicians have joined me in this effort. We just want to connect to our audience honestly, with nothing in between, nothing added and nothing taken away. We are art-ist led. We want the music we make to be heard as we hear it. Music is our life, why would we want less for anyone else? Pono is a journey, an unfolding story. It is just beginning, we are on Chapter One. It won't be finished this month or this year, but along the way we have the opportunity to work together to bring the music back for all of us. Like you John, many people report that they spontaneously dance when they hear music through a PonoPlayer. That is what music does when it is real, that is why we need it. It makes us move. Music is universal, it belongs to all of us, it connects all of us. It transcends us and joins us. We are one.

This is what motivates and drives everyone at Pono. We just want the music back. That makes us human.

Mahalo,
Neil Young
President
Pono Music

Negative criticism of Pono resulted from several factors all too common today and familiar to many companies that bring new products to market. First, skepticism, because people often believe they're being taken advantage of; and second, some have a propensity to criticize pretty much everything. Then there were those who were uncomfortable having their satisfaction with low-res music questioned and not wanting to pay more for high-res music. Reviewers and blog writers, like writers elsewhere on the internet, are motivated by creating controversy to gain more clicks for their articles, which results in generating more advertising dollars. So, they often create headlines to startle, surprise, and grab attention. That's not to say there weren't valid reasons to criticize Pono by those who disliked a small display or the form factor—but certainly not for its audio performance, which was exceptional by all objective standards.

The Pono team was more disappointed by the criticism than upset, because we all knew, based on the facts, that the Pono was a unique product and an accomplishment we all took pride in. We knew the truth, even if others didn't.

The message we responded with was that not all products are for everyone. Pono's intent is to raise the audio standards and provide a means to enjoy it. Pono is not meant to compete with the convenience of streaming. In fact, just the opposite. Higher-quality audio is traded for convenience. It's an alternative way to listen to music for those who can appreciate it. For those who can't, or who don't care, that's fine with us.

Chapter 20 | Phil

CES

The Consumer Electronics Show, held in Las Vegas each January, is the event that nearly every company developing such products attends with great anticipation. It's where they debut their latest creations, and where more than 150,000 people from around the world travel to see them.

CES 2015 would be our first opportunity to present Pono to the worldwide press and create more exposure. Its timing was fortuitous, coming a month after fulfilling our Kickstarter orders, and just as our music store went from beta to 1.0.

We had a small exhibit space at the show and the use of a small conference room at Harman International's exhibit space at the Hard Rock Hotel. Harman, one of the world's largest audio hardware companies (now a part of Samsung), offered the space as a result of some talks that had been ongoing for a few months. The discussions began when Neil met with Harman's CEO, Dinesh Paliwal, to discuss the possibility of the companies working together. Pono needed an investment and we thought Harman might benefit from Pono's efforts in high-quality audio.

On the surface, there seemed to be a lot of opportunities. Harman had strong marketing capabilities, with their audio products being sold globally under a number of brands, and the company was one of the primary designers and suppliers of audio systems to the auto companies. We envisioned Pono electronics and music being incorporated in cars and thought Harman could work with us on future hardware products. Discussions proceeded during the intervening time, and there were plans for a high-level meeting at the end of CES to see if we could negotiate some sort of a deal.

Pedram Abrari at CES 2015

The CES show opened with Neil appearing on the cover of the *CES Daily*, the show's official publication. Neil held a press conference and spoke with reporters covering the event from around the world, generating dozens of stories in magazines, newspapers, and on the web. The press was much kinder to Neil and Pono than the earlier reviews from the tech press, particularly after listening to the demos.

Toward the end of the five-day show, a meeting was held between Pono and Harman to try to strike a deal. Harman agreed to invest about two million dollars, consisting mostly of providing engineers to help Pono develop follow-on products. In exchange, they wanted Neil to endorse and support all of their products, not just Pono, via ads, personal appearances, and other marketing activities.

Having to endorse any and all products was something Neil could not agree to do, although he did agree if it were just Pono. He had no interest in becoming, as Elliot described it, "the Joe DiMaggio of audio," recalling how DiMaggio endorsed Mr. Coffee. Neil has never endorsed a product for money that he didn't believe in and wasn't about to start now, no matter what the investment was. As a result, we failed to come to an agreement.

This was a big disappointment to Pedram, who had worked so hard to try to craft a deal, and it became a turning point for him. He had thought a partnership with Harman would provide a way forward. When it did not, he lost confidence in the future success of Pono, so when a new opportunity came along, he decided to leave a few months later.

Chapter 21 | Neil

CARS AND HIGH RES

When I wanted to demo Pono music to my artist friends, I did it in my car because it provided an ideal environment for listening to music. I've always loved listening while driving, because of how good music can sound and how few other distractions there are. You don't need fancy equipment, just a quality stereo analog amp and a few speakers, typically two in the front, two in the rear, and a subwoofer. Traveling down the road listening to music as the world flies by is one of my great joys.

For my Pono demos, I used an analog system in my seventies Cadillac. I used just the stock speakers that were in it, feeding various resolutions to the analog amp and speakers. Pure. I did have a good analog amp in the trunk feeding those speakers, but I didn't change the speakers. I didn't want to tear the car apart.

Of the hundred or so artists who listened to the Pono demos, choosing the resolutions they could listen to "on the fly" and comparing without stopping the music, 98 percent chose high-resolution listening over all of the other formats. These included CD, MP3, Apple files, and others. That was a straight-up listening comparison and the choices were conclusive. Artists definitely can feel the difference, but it's a difference everyone can feel, although some may not be able to recognize it in a test situation. It's a feeling over time. The more you hear, the more you recognize the value of good-sounding music. You *feel* it. That is what music is. It is subtle but huge.

Today, all of the audio systems in cars are digital, as is the music. However, rather than using a high-quality DAC to convert digital music to analog at the source and using analog components to amplify it and drive the speakers, manufacturers do something much different. Unfortunately for music, it sounds pretty bad.

I visited a number of auto manufacturers for discussions about the deteriorating audio quality in automobiles. I'll give you a few examples of my own experiences.

LINCOLN

I had been corresponding with Alan Norton in the Lincoln division of Ford Motors, who worked on their car audio systems and was investigating how to bring high-res sound and better audio to the future Lincoln models. I liked Alan, and he was encouraging. He contacted me after he bought a Pono, writing about how much he loved its sound, and inviting me out to meet the head of the Lincoln division and the audio team. They wanted to show me what they were doing to try to integrate a Pono player in one of their cars.

I was excited and flew to Ford's headquarters in Dearborn, Michigan, for a visit. We all met in a huge conference room, and I remember it well. There were a lot of folks, people from Lincoln's audio equipment manufacturer and experienced Ford people. One of their assistants brought Starbucks coffee to everyone. This was about the same time my targeted recording "A Rock Star Bucks a Coffee Shop" was released, criticizing Starbucks for supporting the repeal of the Vermont law requiring GMO disclosures on foods. Of course, I was polite and didn't say anything—but I didn't drink the coffee.

The Lincoln team described the audio system they were working on. They talked about how feature-populated it was. The system was based on digital technology, with many new features that I thought had no real connection to truc audio quality. For example, they explained that the speakers had to be "time-aligned" because the car is moving fast. The speakers have to be corrected as the car travels, so that sound gets to the back of the car at just the right time, or something like that. They described how the playback also needs to be time-aligned and balanced because of the characteristics and shapes inside of the car. Their solution required each speaker set to have its own converter to go from digital to analog and would use a digital signal processing chip and a digital amplifier chip to process the audio signals. The solution, I understood, was different-sized speakers for different areas of the car.

Thinking about the car audio presentation, I tried to keep an open mind. In my purist view, this was completely bogus. First, you would not be driving anywhere near the speed of sound for there to be any difference from the front of the car to the back.

Second, I felt the extra components compromised the sound; even if they made a difference with effects, they started out with inferior sound right out of the gate. I'm sure they believed some of this was an improvement, but they were presenting ideas and concepts that made little sense to me.

In my way of thinking, for the best audio quality, signal processing should only be done once, while going from the digital file to the analog amplification that drives the speakers. Because they utilized so many cheap DACs and low-cost digital amplifier chips in so many places throughout the car to enable "features," replacing them all with really good ones would be too expensive. It would have sounded better and been much cheaper if they had used just one top-quality DAC to feed high-quality analog amplifiers.

The entire architecture of their car, all of these special effects that they described, and the number of speakers were pushed by their designers and component manufacturers, but were just there to make them and their customers think that they're getting something more.

It's great marketing, but it has nothing to do with the quality of the sound. While they could use many digital features to change the soundstage to resemble a concert hall, boost the bass to create a rumble, or any number of things, none of that provided better audio. The components just made it sound more degraded, more synthetic. The system was polishing a turd. That's why, today, new cars just don't sound as good as they used to. Digital overkill.

I mean, it's weird. I used to be able to listen to an AM radio in a car and get more out of the music than I get out of any of the new cars today.

More real sound. More music. More feelings.

PONO IN A CAR

After the engineers described what they were doing, we all went downstairs to a test car in their lab to listen to their system and try out Pono. I asked them not to use their existing digital amplifiers, DACs, or any of their sound-shaping systems. Just play the Pono's high-resolution music directly through an analog amp that was wired to a few of the crucial speakers.

They connected the Pono and everyone took turns getting in the car and listening. Many seemed surprised by how good it sounded. We tried a bunch of songs, including mine, some from Adele, and some of their test files. They really appeared awed by it. It seemed eye opening for the engineers, who knew mostly digital and were wedded to it because of all of the tricks you can do with it.

In my mind, superfluous features are the killer of quality. Pure design is the savior.

The Lincoln engineers were smart people but had less understanding of analog audio in this age where everything is digital. Because digital had given them all of these options, they took it to the extreme, and even did something I would never have imagined: they superimposed a special background sound over the audio.

All the music had a drone in it!

Driving as I listened to their sound system, I recognized that something didn't sound right; something was muddying up the audio. When I asked them about this, they explained that they had simulated the sound of an eight-cylinder engine in the background to create the effect of a more powerful car, masking the real sound from the car's four-cylinder engine.

I saw what I was up against.

It was crazy. How did that improve audio quality?

TESLA

But it was not only Ford who didn't get their audio right. I tried to explain some of this to Tesla creator Elon Musk. I wanted him to set up a Pono system in one of his cars. I wanted to tear apart a Tesla and then rebuild it with new components, and then have him compare it to a new Tesla, the way they're building it now, because I knew it would sound so much better—so obvious that you couldn't miss it.

When I started talking to him about this, he told me that a Tesla is a digital machine. What he meant is that he and his engineers like the bells and whistles, they like all the back-and-forth manipulation and controls that digital enables. It's like driving a phone.

Of course, it is possible to use digital controls for analog sound and get the best of both worlds. I tried explaining that simple approach to their audio engineers, and when they discovered what I was getting into, they couldn't wait to get rid of me. In essence, I was eliminating their jobs. When I spoke directly to Elon, I tried to explain to him that if I could just get audio from the Pono player to the speakers in his car through a wire that plugs in, just to demonstrate it, he would be able to hear the difference as opposed to the signal processing he was using. The sound would live up to the Tesla name.

"Let's just try using some analog amps and plug in a Pono!" I said. That was what I wanted to show him and let him feel.

But Elon got distracted by the fact that in my "demo" there was a wire that would plug in, and said, "Oh, we can't have a wire." He dismissed me completely because of the wire, only there to make a simple demo.

I don't believe he's that stupid. That wasn't it. I figured that he just wanted to get rid of me, and he thought he was already doing a brilliant job with sound. I wasn't impressed with his lack of willingness to admit that anything could be wrong with his car. It was disappointing that he didn't want to learn how to improve his great piece of automotive engineering (and it is). But I couldn't get through to him. It was like his way was great, and what they already had was the best.

He kept saying, "We're the best. We get all the awards. We're the best-sounding car."

And I was going, "Yeah, you're the best-sounding car and you have an MP3 player in the car? You gotta be kidding me."

I wanted Tesla to be in another league, as it is with power. But Elon just didn't get it. A lot of people are like that; they can be brilliant in electronics, brilliant in software, and just very brilliant people. He is. But they sometimes don't get this. Music. Not everyone hears it. But given a chance, they would *feel* it.

It's quite interesting that the leaders of these companies can't—or don't want to—hear the difference. But I can hear the difference and I know through math and through physics that analog audio is better. The fewer things you do to the sound, the better it is. Less is more. This philosophy doesn't work with many of today's products. To them, more is more. If it's crap, more crap is better than just a little bit of crap. So, they decorate it.

Someday, if I ever have another big hit record (ha ha), I'll buy a Tesla and dismantle it, replacing the sound system with one of my own design. I will take it back to Elon and show him what it feels like to hear quality sound in his beautiful quiet car. That would be *my* Tesla.

With the car manufacturers, I learned that there's little thought given to the idea of "let's simplify and make it straight-forward." That way of thinking is gone . . . for now.

If you put four or six, maybe eight speakers in a car, in the right places, and a subwoofer, and a stereo amp to drive it, it's completely awesome. It's unbelievable. But no, the digital feature engineers think twenty speakers are better than five, and thirty speakers are better than twenty.

Trying to turn technology into products that can grow and reproduce, to just keep putting more and more superfluous and quality-inhibiting features into those products, is not the way real technology works. I think technology is supposed to be something that serves you to make your life better, to improve lives. Today's cars are a blatant example of technology not doing that. Complexity is mistaken for progress.

You know, I may end up going to my grave and be banging my head against my gravestone trying to get somebody to under-stand about what's happening to music! I've thought about that more and more as time goes by, that no one hears the degradation of sound. No one but the hundred artists who listened to Pono in my 1978 Cadillac, including Elton John, Stephen Stills, Norah Jones, and countless other superb musicians. Norah said, "This makes listening fun again!" Time and time again, artists chose high-resolution digital through analog amplification unanimously over all other options.

So, I'm not giving up. This is too important to give up on. I trust artists.

Chapter 22 | Phil

BUILD IT AND WAIT

As challenging as it is to develop and manufacture a product, the path to commercial success can often be much more difficult, and often much more expensive. And that was true with Pono. Few products have succeeded by just announcing their arrival.

Despite limited financial resources, we had come a long way, much further than many startups do. We had turned an idea into a credible product that filled a need at an attractive price. We had a great player and a unique music store devoted to high-res downloads.

RETAIL CHALLENGE

But we had an even bigger task in front of us: turning Pono into a sustainable business. Over the next few months we set up our retail distribution in the US and Canada. We brought in a sales executive, James Berberian, who had headed up sales for Targus, a computer accessory company, in its early years. Berberian had great relations with the resellers and was responsible for Targus's meteoric growth. Along with Sami Kamangar, he reached out to a number of resellers—physical, catalogs, and online—to sell and promote the Pono player. Our largest and most successful reseller was, not surprisingly, Amazon. Others included B&H in New York City, Fry's, Crutchfield, London Drug of Canada, and a number of independent audio and record stores. With the growth of Amazon and the shrinking retail space, we encountered many of the challenges that most small consumer electronics companies face.

Our first goal was to get visibility at retail stores, so shoppers could discover, listen to, and hopefully buy Pono players. Retailers typically demand payments for shelf space and for their own advertising. They also insist on being able to return a product that doesn't sell, and they often take sixty to ninety days to pay for those products that do. Essentially, you're providing the products on consignment. Amazon is the exception. They take a smaller cut and pay much more promptly. While many of us prefer to shop at Amazon for convenience, many companies sell on Amazon to avoid the retailers.

In addition to the major retailers, Neil wanted to support local record stores that were seeing a resurgence of vinyl sales. We provided free demo players to selected record stores so that their customers could try them out.

Unfortunately, we were hampered by a tiny marketing budget that didn't allow us to advertise and limited what we could do within retail stores. Ideally, we'd want to provide an automated demo station that would allow customers to easily sample music, but we could only afford to provide a demo player and some simple signage. While we could get players into stores, sell-through was modest and most of our sales came from Amazon, Fry's, and our own site, much of it driven through word of mouth and owner referrals.

SELLING DOWNLOADS

As more units were sold, sales from our music download store began to grow and became a steady source of income, but still far less than what we needed to support the continued development costs of the store. For every dollar in download sales, our gross profit was thirty cents, a formula established by the music industry for all companies selling downloads.

Because we were working on such a small budget, we had insufficient funds to do what we would have liked to do, which was to launch a PR and advertising campaign to create demand for the product and to improve retail sell-through. Liam Casey offered us some short-term help and provided several of his company's PR people to help us launch.

Yet "Build it and they will come" rarely works, even when it's Neil Young. Certainly, the mixed reviews from tech reviewers and bloggers didn't help, but what seemed to be the greatest resistance to sales was that users simply did not want to give up the convenience of streaming on their phone, even in exchange for much better sound. By the first half of 2015, Spotify, Pandora, and

YouTube soared to one-third of all revenues from recorded music, while CD sales were dropping rapidly.

For the next nine months, Pono continued to grow slowly, with download sales reaching $3,000 to $5,000 per day. But we were still cash poor and spending loads of money on running and maintaining the music store.

Neil's persistence and strong belief in the cause of quality audio—and, equally important, his and his friends' financial support—kept us alive. Some of us worked for deferred payment and some employees chose to leave. But we maintained a core team consisting of Rick Cohen, Randy Leasure, Kevin Fielding, Damani Jackson, Zeke Young, Sami Kamangar, myself, and a couple of consultants. Randy picked up some of the work Pedram had been doing and managed our music store and our relations with

Kevin Fielding, Elliot, and Neil

the labels, including creating weekly promotions to continue to build its sales.

MANAGEMENT CHANGE

Rick Cohen eventually left, precipitated by his contentious interaction with our manufacturer, Liam Casey, who could no longer work with Cohen.

Neil stepped back in as CEO and asked me to become COO. My main role was to try to stabilize the organization and keep us in business. We were resigned to taking the long view and building the business slowly but steadily. This was Neil's preference all along. We even had defined Pono 2, a refinement of the original Pono player that would add several new features, such as Wi-Fi to make downloading music easier and incorporating new circuitry that Charley Hansen had designed to make the player sound even better.

We managed to survive all of this time, nearly two years, while Elliot worked closely with our suppliers to negotiate new terms and keep them engaged. Foremost on his mind was protecting Neil's reputation and avoiding bankruptcy. It had to be one of the most difficult jobs that I could imagine anyone doing. Elliot never wavered from trying to keep the company alive and to support Neil's goals while hoping for an upturn.

We were running on a shoestring, and susceptible to any adverse event, such as the one that was about to hit us.

Chapter 23 | Phil

THAT OMINOUS CALL

*I*n May 2016 we received a call from Omnifone, the provider of all the back-end services for our music store, telling us that they had just filed for bankruptcy. They reassured us that they would continue to run their operations and our business would not be affected. Clearly, that made us nervous, but there was little we could do.

We were right to have been concerned. A month later, Omnifone received an offer to be purchased. They called to tell us that they would be shutting down all operations within the next four days, including our store—a requirement of their buyer, Apple. That was a devastating blow to Pono that impacted our entire business model and extinguished a key source of our revenue. The store was instrumental to the Pono business. The loss of Omnifone meant that we would lose access to all of the content of our music store. We could no longer sell downloads. Our source of music delivery was cut off.

Neil tried calling Eddie Cue, Apple's executive who ran all of the company's music services, but was never able to reach him. He left several messages, but Cue never called back.

So, did Apple buy Omnifone simply to shut them down and to put us out of business? At the time, the rumors were that they did it to get access to Omnifone's employees and technology, but either way, we were collateral damage. We had no other choice than to look for an alternative company to develop our music store, starting all over again from scratch. As we searched, we expected that the closure of our music store would be temporary.

There was only one practical alternative, a company called 7digital, also based in the UK. We reached out to them and quickly came to an agreement. One of the requirements was for them to rebuild the entire music library that we lost from Omnifone and incorporate all the features that made the Pono music store so unique: highlighting high-res albums; eliminating all lower-res content that was available in higher-res; running promotions; and, of course, incorporating the Pono Promise, allowing free upgrades when a higher-res version became available. They had assured us that this development work was straightforward and could be done quickly.

However, as we began working together and got into the specific details, 7digital found the cost to implement these changes to be much higher than they originally estimated, and that it would take much more time than they had assumed. While we could have used their generic store design, it would have been just like all the other download stores, with none of the features that had made our store so special by focusing on high res.

PONO COMES TO AN END

After examining the amount of sales that we'd need to cover the 7digital development costs, the numbers just didn't work. We had finally met a challenge that we couldn't overcome.

Apple's sudden closing of Omnifone was certainly not the only cause of Pono's demise, but it was the final event that led to Pono deciding to shut down. Neil announced the sad news in a letter posted on the Pono website at the end of December 2017:

Ladies and Gentlemen:

As you all know, we have been working to bring high-quality music back to the world that's become used to mediocre, hollowed-out files. The cause seemed to be a win-win for everyone. The artists would allow their fans to hear what they hear in the studios, and the music lovers would hear the music the best it could be. This cause has been something I've written and talked about for over twenty years. I cared and I assumed that most of the world would care.

It's been almost five years since we kicked off the campaign at SXSW to offer a player and download content that could fulfill my dream of bringing to you a music experience unlike any other for the cost. Thanks to our supporters on Kickstarter, the follow-on customers and some very good friends that supported the effort, we delivered on that promise. Our player won best digital portable product of the year from Stereophile magazine, and we offered some of the best high-resolution content to be found anywhere. We sold tens of thousands of players, every unit that we made. Thanks for that!

But, despite that success, I was not satisfied. I had to put up with lots of criticism for the high cost of music delivered in the way all music should be provided, at full resolution and not hollowed out. I had no control over the pricing, but I was the one that felt the criticism, because I was the face of it. And I pretty much agreed with the criticism. Music should not be priced this way.

When Omnifone, our download store partner, was bought and shut down with no notice by Apple, we began work with another company to build the same download store. But the more we worked on it, the more we realized how difficult it would be to recreate what we had and how costly it was to run it: to deliver the Pono Promise, meaning you'd never have to buy the same album again if it was released at a higher quality; the ability to access just high-res music, and not the same performances at lower quality, and the ability to do special sales. Each of these features was expensive to implement.

I also realized that just bringing back the store was not enough. While there was a dedicated audience, I could not in good conscience continue to justify the higher costs. When it comes to high res, the record industry is still broken. The industry was such that even when I wanted to remaster some of the great performances from my artist friends at high res, Pono had to pay thousands of dollars for each recording, with little expectation of getting the money back. Record companies believe they should charge a premium for high-res recordings and conversely, I believe all music should cost the same, regardless of the technology used.

As you might imagine, we found it difficult to raise more money for this model: delivering quality music at a premium price to a limited audience that felt they were being taken advantage of with the high costs.

Additionally, the company was in default on its loans of over $2.5 million in the aggregate to its secured creditors, who moved to foreclose on the assets.

In light of the challenges facing Pono and the financial condition of the company, the Board of Directors acknowledged that it was time to wind down and dissolve the company . . .

Thank you all very much for supporting Pono and quality audio.

Very truly yours,
Ivanhoe (DE) Inc.
Neil Young
President
Elliott Roberts
Secretary

Chapter 29 | Neil

THE END OF PONO?

Taking on the status quo is never an easy task. We were up against an established and convenient way of hearing music that had ingrained itself in the public consciousness and was accepted across the board.

Having to shutter our Pono business was a giant disappointment to me and to all of our Pono supporters, employees, and investors. We spent so much time, effort, and money to do what we believed and still believe to be so important. Our vision resonated with numerous investors who made contributions to support what we all believed in, and I met like-minded people wherever I went who thanked me for our efforts. I am grateful to all for their support. I'm convinced Pono's existence was a very important step toward the goal of improving the audio quality of music and bringing back the *feeling*—just not the last step.

THE PONO EFFECT

Pono raised awareness way beyond the audiophile community and encouraged discussions about audio quality, even controversial ones, among the media. While we were never able to get actual competitive sales data, we believe that, in its first year, more Pono music players were sold than any other brand, and that our download store was selling a greater percentage of high-res content than anyone else. We became synonymous with quality audio and the destination for high-res downloads.

FIRST TO BRING HIGH-RESOLUTION MUSIC TO THE MASSES

Before Pono, high-res music players had been focused on audiophiles. Pono was the first to bring a high-quality player and high-res music to the mainstream music lover. It was easier to use and offered better performance than any other player. But it was not a phone.

Pono created a community with tens of thousands of supporters worldwide. They bought players and downloads and contributed to our vibrant and growing community forum. Each of them became an advocate for our mission. Now, even though our music store is gone, high-res downloads continue to be available from other sites around the world and play on Pono players to the delight of their owners.

NOT PROPRIETARY

Pono never used a proprietary file format or limited what you could do with the downloads our customers bought, something the industry is once more attempting to do indirectly by using Meridian's MQA compression scheme. While I applaud the industry's effort here to offer higher quality, using a proprietary format that manipulates the audio and requires compatible hardware is shortsighted and another costly and greedy mistake by the record companies supporting it. I don't think that will ever work. It comes at a big cost.

Pono was able to demonstrate to the tech industry that a small team could deliver a solution far superior in its audio quality and simpler to use than what anyone else was offering.

HIGH RES

More companies are now embracing high res, following Pono's lead. Sony introduced a line of affordable high-res players and a high-res initiative across many of their products, putting listening stations into retail stores to demonstrate its benefits. New players were introduced by Onkyo, FiiO, Shure, and Astell&Kern. There are even a few smartphones such as top-of-the-line LG and Samsung models that have built-in high-res music players. Even among the streaming services there's a movement, albeit slow, to improve quality. Tidal offers streaming with near-CD quality and

MQA; Qobuz, a French company, is offering high-res streaming; and Murfie is offering a service to stream their customers' vinyl records and CDs at their full resolution.

Did they all do it because of Pono? Not entirely, but we certainly raised awareness, and brought in educated new customers who better understand the advantages. The Pono player has become the gold standard, the product many audio reviewers still use as the benchmark to measure new players, asking "How does it compare with Pono?" or "Is it as good as Pono?"

VINYL

Quality music is making a comeback. It's a slow one. In addition to the proliferation of quality music players, we've seen a revival of vinyl sales for both my albums and those of my artist friends, and it now accounts for one of the industry's largest areas of growth. It's certainly not because of convenience. I think it's mostly because of vinyl's amazing audio quality. A note of caution, though: all vinyl is not equal. If it comes from the analog master, it will be great. If it comes from a high-resolution file, it could also be great. If it comes from a CD, mastered through a super-high-end DAC, then it will be better than a CD, but nowhere near legacy analog vinyl or high-resolution vinyl quality.

STREAMING MUSIC

Over the years, my friend and former Pono board member Gigi Brisson often said to me, "Neil, can't we try streaming?"

I would reply, "There's nobody who can stream the true quality of music."

As I said, I was wrong. That was one of my biggest mistakes, not listening to Gigi. She was not limited by her technical knowledge and recognized that high-res streaming would be of huge value. I was in a technical box and was sure that streaming technology couldn't do it. It hadn't been done at that time, and it would take a few more years before the problems that kept it from being practical were solved. I was blind to that.

As an artist, I objected to streaming for many reasons. Streaming was disrupting the industry. Record companies were making all these new deals with streaming companies that many artists could not understand. It became clear that streaming was a boon to record companies, bringing them a windfall at the expense of the artists, who suffered when streaming replaced physical media.

With streaming, the person who wrote the song gets paid, but those who performed on the record get very little or nothing. The digital age has made it possible to cut out the original artists from the profit chain. With that happening, there was really no reason for artists to continue to try to create music if they couldn't make a living from it.

The industry's answer to the artists' loss of revenue was for the artists to make their living by just doing live performances. That was Silicon Valley's answer, too. We're giving away your music, taking away your income from selling your recordings, but you can make a living playing live. In 2017, the artists who actually created the music got just 12 percent of the music industry's $43 billion in revenue. This is the new age of digital music.

I really wanted to make music sound better, and I thought it was something I could do with my life, something of significance. While I've made some other contributions, what I saw going on with music, with the quality going downhill, was just so disheartening. I felt I had to do something. I couldn't listen to my own music anymore, my own recordings. I only listen to what I get at the end of a day's recording session to check on its quality. No one else gets to hear that anymore.

Looking back, I assumed that streaming would never be able to get to the level of high res, so we went in the direction of high-res downloads and a great music player. But as I said, one of my biggest mistakes was a failure to recognize sooner the impact of streaming and how fast it would replace CDs and downloads. In fact, its impact on the record companies has been so significant that it has kept many of them in the black. My aversion to streaming was not only because of its effect on music quality but because of how poorly record companies and streaming deals treat the artists. That's another story, and it's not a good one.

In spite of my personal feelings, streaming cannot be ignored, and to attain my goals I should have taken it more seriously. John Hamm, a few years earlier, had brought up the idea and told me about a company in Asia that was working on technology to improve streaming quality, but we were in the midst of Pono and we never pursued it. That was a big mistake.

OPPORTUNITY

During one of my last visits to the Pono office in San Francisco, I met with our small team and let them know that we couldn't justify investing more money to rebuild our download music store. The discussions then turned to streaming. Kevin Fielding, our software engineer, mentioned that a tiny company in Singapore had just created a high-res streaming service that was providing Sony classical music at CD and higher quality. They had developed a way to send music over both slow and fast networks, providing the best audio quality possible all the time, depending on the bandwidth available to the listener.

The streamed audio files would be compressed in size—in real time—to work on slow networks and adjust to constantly changing conditions. That meant it would work like current streaming services when the bandwidth was limited but could change to CD quality or higher res, seamlessly, when the bandwidth allowed. At the highest level it would play full high resolution, with no compression. They called it adaptive streaming, and they had been working on it for years, building it on top of an unused industry standard. The bandwidth in some areas is now so high that full high-resolution streaming could be possible at last. I couldn't get it out of my mind.

The firm, OraStream, was the same company Hamm had told me about. Interestingly, Hamm had found us Charley Hansen (the designer of Pono) long ago and had also found OraStream (the solution to high-res streaming) before I "discovered" it. I wished I had recognized these things right away.

ORASTREAM

When OraStream streamed a music file, it would send a tiny bit of test data to determine the speed of the network and then send the highest possible quality file from among its 15,000 levels, matching its resolution to the available bandwidth. High-speed networks would get high res and slow-speed networks might get MP3 quality. This was all done inaudibly using the industry-standard FLAC file format.

I was very excited by what they had done and asked Phil to investigate and learn more. Phil contacted Frankie Tan, the founder, and confirmed that it worked with all resolutions, although many of their users were listening to CD-quality music, because of the paucity of high-res music.

The company provided us data showing how the service was being used among its subscribers. It showed the average bandwidth used by listeners in many different cities where they received their streaming music. The same music was being experienced from high res in some locations to low-res MP3 quality or below in others, but it all originated from one file. Adaptive streaming has been used in video for years. That's what makes Netflix possible. But it had been pretty much ignored for audio.

My instant reaction was to see if we could use OraStream to develop a high-resolution streaming service. I became very excited by the possibilities. I realized that it would take a huge effort and a lot of money. It meant starting over completely. I thought of the famous quote from Alexander Graham Bell: "When one door closes, another opens."

And I thought about John Hamm.

Chapter 25 | Neil

STREAMING IN HIGH RES

*I*was intrigued by OraStream's adaptive streaming technology. It seemed to be a much better approach than what the industry was doing. Imagine, a single music file that could self-adjust in 15,000 steps between MP3 and high resolution, depending on the customer's listening situation—their available bandwidth.

Compare that to existing streaming services still using old technology—tiny MP3 audio files that stream at either 160 or 320 kbps, sometimes even less. Now compare that with high res that streams at 5,000 to 6,000 kbps, delivering more than twenty times the information.

When I had discussed streaming quality with some of the people running the streaming services, they would tell me that they don't offer better-quality streaming because it wouldn't work for those customers who have slow connection speeds. Therefore, the streaming companies opted to give everyone music at a quality that's determined by the worst conditions. Those days and needs are over.

TRAGEDY

Not only does that streaming approach deprive most of us of good audio, but it's conditioning those who listen using only streaming to believe that this is what music is all about. They've not heard anything better and have no idea of what they're missing. That is a real tragedy.

The other objection to high res, the streaming companies would tell me, is that a customer would have to pay more for their data if they were using a cellular connection. High res uses more data.

Okay, there is some truth to this if the customer is using cellular and not Wi-Fi. A subscriber listening to high res could exhaust their data allowance much faster, depending on their cellular plan. But an OraStream file could simply be switched to play at old-school low res in those circumstances and use no more data. Or they could leave it full-on, hear all the music, and *feel* its magic. It's the user's choice. A real choice.

ONE FILE AND THE END OF FORMATS

The end of formats satisfies all customers, those who think they need the small files and low resolution because of poor connections or data limitations, as well as those who want to listen to high res in their homes over a fast Wi-Fi network. They'd be able to listen to a single file for any given recording. A user could listen on their phone in their car at a low resolution, and then arrive home with Wi-Fi and listen at high resolution seamlessly.

Having one file for all resolutions even makes things easier for the streaming companies. Currently, they must buy different files from the record companies for each resolution level they offer, such as 160 and 320 kbps.

IMPROVING STREAMING

What I don't understand is why the industry doesn't advance its streaming as the technology evolves. They do it in all other areas of tech. They've been using the first-generation streaming going well into its second decade, so isn't it time to improve it? Ora-Stream is the next generation of streaming—positioned for the future, particularly as faster networks, 5G, and less expensive data plans become available.

OraStream told me they had met with some of the major record companies and that their technology had been well received. The labels had tested it and liked it but had little incentive to push it at a time when the existing streaming services were finally making them profitable.

I really wanted to support OraStream because of the big impact it would have on improving audio quality. I believed that it could be the basis for a new generation of streaming service. I even invested my own money in the struggling company to keep it alive.

The best outcome would be for one of the streaming services to adopt it, but OraStream had little success in their efforts to get any of them interested. When I reached out to my contacts in these companies, I got much the same response. What I found was some curiosity and interest, but I also found audio quality not to be a big enough reason for any of them to make changes to what they thought was good enough. They either just didn't know better or they didn't really care.

Meanwhile, we went to work testing the OraStream technology to become more familiar with all its capabilities, limitations, and issues. It performed well in most situations, but we continuously came up with ways to make it work even better. That was really exciting!

Because there were so few high-res recordings available, much of OraStream's previous work had been based on optimizing their streaming service for mostly CD quality. As noted, just before the start of every album play, they test the network to determine the optimal resolution. It starts at 160 kbps to work everywhere, and then increases within a few seconds to the appropriate level. I wanted to reduce the time for the music to reach 192/24. I worked with OraStream engineers to add some intelligence and to alter the algorithms to do such things as remembering the results of previous network queries. That allowed the music to ramp up even faster and, in some cases, avoided the need to test the network. We also added a mode in which streaming would be done at a fixed low resolution for those worst-case situations. Finally, after months of testing in early 2017, we were really pleased at how well the service worked, and we named it "Xstream."

A PLAN

That was when I decided that we needed to write a business plan for this new high-res streaming service. I had no illusions about the difficulty of getting folks interested in another streaming service. I hadn't forgotten about my experience with Pono. It would mean needing to raise many tens of millions of dollars just to get the service off the ground. I'd need a CEO and employees.

I wanted to at least be able to create a plan to present to the record companies, the tech industry, and potential investors to see if I could generate some interest.

My goal was to promote and expose this new technology and to put my name and reputation behind it, because it had the potential to change the face of streaming and remove consumer music's major limitation of poor audio quality. We could have the convenience of streaming with the benefits of high res. That was my mission, more important to me than creating another company.

I worked with Elliot, Phil, and Rob Bikel, a strategy consultant and professor at Pepperdine University, to write a business plan. (Rob was referred to me by my friend Michael Crooke, also a professor there.) I also got help from Bob Gunderson and Jeff Thacker, lawyers from a Silicon Valley law firm with experience in funding startup businesses, to reach out to potential investors and partners.

Unlike Spotify, Tidal, Pandora, and other streaming services that marketed directly to users, I envisioned Xstream as a streaming service that we'd offer to select industry players. Apple focused on the quality of its camera to sell its mobile phone. Some of the cellular providers offered free video streaming. Xstream would try to find companies that wanted to be the first to offer high-res audio streaming to their customers.

I reached out to the Canadian cellular companies, Rogers and Bell Canada, and explained how they could offer their own streaming service, powered by Xstream, that would be so much better than any music streaming offering elsewhere. I offered to provide my entire archive of recorded musical performances, going all the way back to the early 1960s, exclusively to Xstream users to encourage adoption.

We got some interest, but the companies moved really slowly, and we never made much progress. One liked it, but the agreement they had with one of the streaming companies wouldn't allow them to work with a second. They were locked into low quality. Honestly, it was a frustrating experience.

One incident I remember is when I drove down to San Diego and Jeff Thacker took us to meet with the investment people at Qualcomm. Jeff and I thought high-res music was a perfect match for the 5G technology they were developing for the cellular industry. But the meeting was disappointing. A huge group came in to hear me discuss the state of music quality, and how 5G could have a huge impact in delivering great audio, but most just sat quietly with little emotion. When I was finished and answered a few questions, one of their executives took me back to his office, not to discuss what I just presented but to take a selfie with me. They were clueless.

PRICED RIGHT

For Xstream to be viable, it had to be priced right. The industry was already charging premium pricing for higher quality streaming such as Jay-Z's Tidal, priced at $20 a month for near-CD quality compared to everyone else's MP3 for $10 a month.

I thought that was crazy—it was the same mistake that record companies had made when pricing downloads, and they keep doing it over and over again. I wanted all streaming to be priced the same at $10 per month. I knew that was low and would be difficult for the record companies to accept. They would see Xstream as a way to charge more because of its high-res capabilities, even when customers might use it at low res. We needed to get them to think in a different way when it came to pricing if Xstream was to have any chance of succeeding.

I decided to meet face-to-face with the heads of the labels to explain to them about Xstream and to convince them how it could benefit the industry. But I didn't want to sell it as high res, which would lead to high prices. Instead I called it "all res."

In January 2017, I flew to New York City with Elliot and Phil to meet with the executives of Warner, Universal, and Sony—the three companies that I needed to convince. We had meetings with Michele Anthony of Universal, Dennis Kooker and Mark Piibe of Sony, and Steve Cooper and Ole Obermann at Warner and explained the technology and then discussed the pricing.

I got good responses from everyone. They understood. While there was little awareness of our technology among these executives, they all thought it made sense.

But there was also an attitude within these large organizations to keep things as they were. That's what the music industry has become: more interested in survival due to the turbulent times they've gone through, and happy with the success they're finally seeing from the streaming services.

HI-RES STREAMING FOR $10/MONTH

I explained that I thought Xstream needed to be priced at $10 to have any chance of immediate success. We couldn't repeat the model used for Tidal and price it high. That made no sense because Xstream was used at all resolutions, not just high. It depended on what bandwidth was available. It might be extremely low. You can't overcharge for lower quality than Spotify. Xstream was a different animal.

Some executives pushed back because they thought it would create problems with the other streaming services. How could they allow a new company with high res to offer better quality at the same price? I kept pushing and explained how this kind of thinking didn't work with downloads and won't work for streaming. We want to provide the best quality at one price. Eventually I made headway, and all but Sony agreed to $10. Sony agreed to $12.99. That is a pretty good price for starters, I thought. I'm not much of a businessman. I wanted this thing to get going and have people hear and feel it. I sensed it could be a *revolution*.

We returned home to California trying to figure out how to move forward with Xstream and to put it to use without more delays.

A DIFFERENT IDEA

While trying to interest investors and find partners was frustrat-ingly slow, I had a different idea: Why not use it on just my own music to show that it could be done? Reduce the pressure of hav-ing to sell the idea to all the companies and artists and raise mil-lions of dollars. High resolution could be streamed, and I could prove it on my own turf, with my own music.

Chapter 26 | Neil

NYA

*L*et me digress a little.

I had given a lot of thought to developing a visual way to look at music in the context of time. One of my first ideas in 1990 was something I called DiscoChron—The Chronology of Music. This was a vague dream, a vision of something like an electromechanical time machine. It was a game with a rolling ball—think of a pinball machine where the ball travels through time, ricocheting through time and space, but every once in a while, it detours in one direction or another, to stop and pick up media and news collected during the period of time you were currently traveling.

The media would be arranged in chronological order, so that as you encounter it, depending on where you are in space and time, you also could view important events in the world that occurred at the same time. You're presented with the history of the world and of our civilization as you listen to the music from that time period. The concept is to go back and forth along this time line: stop here, stop there, pick up media here, pick it up there, and play it back in its purest form.

TIME LINE

It's a very simple concept, and it's not limited just to music. It's art, books, movies, the life and death of presidents, the political history of the world, and even the history of humanity.

It's applicable to other artistic endeavors, such as authors and their books, showing a time line when the books were written along with what was going on in the world at the time. You could find any book that you want to read from among the author's entire writings in one place. If you like an adventure writer like Clive Cussler, you can access the entire Dirk Pitt series from beginning to end, from his very first mention to the last, along with the author's comments about what it was like writing those books. There'd be information about what was going on in the world at that time, as well as personal stories about what was happening while he was writing it—any story the author might want to share. For example, what was involved in creating the cover art and who the artist was, who were the publisher and the editor, who were the people who distributed it, what countries was it sold in.

You could apply this concept to many different things, anything that has a history. Anything that's moving through time that has media associated with it. Your journey through time and space might leave a trace that others could then experience.

THE HISTORY OF MUSIC

What about music? Well, the history of the music would be there for everybody to experience forever, instead of the hodgepodge of bullshit that we have now of MP3s, of people needing to research all of this on their own by going to libraries and doing Google searches, YouTubing, and reading what others wrote. This would be the real thing, and a lot more than just accessing and listening to music; that's just a small part of it. Everything is in one place in its proper context; it's all locked together by time instead of location.

This concept was the genesis of my idea for the Neil Young Archives. Think of the archives as a new kind of scrapbook. It would contain a variety of memorabilia, not just the audio files but also a place where I could explain the development of my lyrics, show photographs, read my notes, and so forth. And it would be indexed in such a way that, as you progressed through it, you could delve deeper into a particular year, a particular album, or whatever.

In 1990, when I started out with my first archives, there was no technology that would allow something like my time machine to be implemented. The internet of the day couldn't have handled it. DVDs never worked because they couldn't handle high-res audio with the large amount of other material I wanted to include, although Blu-ray got us a little closer.

BLU-RAY

Blu-ray discs offered huge storage capacity, but the format was still challenging and clunky. It was like pulling levers and doing all kinds of shit to create them. But it was as close as I could get at the time. It enabled me to have archival material on all these discs, even though the discs had their own drawbacks. You couldn't fly through time as I'd envisioned—you can only do something like a year and then you have to go to another disc, so that was cumbersome. But that was the idea. The whole concept was there; it was just the media and technology that was holding us back. And it was very expensive—$25,000 to create each disc. That's $250,000 to master my entire first Archive Blu-ray set.

When people bought the set, they didn't know exactly what it was. Those who got it went, "Holy shit, what is this thing? This is insane." It still wasn't quite right, it was just an early glimpse of what could happen.

So, while I realized that I could do all this on a website, there was no way to provide the music at the quality I needed. That was when I started thinking, "Well, I can play it back directly from files off the computer and I can also have the entire history of my music along a single time line, so you can move along the line for fifty years without needing to change a disc." I thought that was incredible. Just go anywhere, back and forth, and grab anything, call it up, and zoom in, or slowly cruise there, or whatever you want to do. This was all occurring around the turn of the century, in 2000. That was when we started thinking about doing it on the internet.

We had already released *Archives Vol. 1* on Blu-ray and we were now working on *Vol. 2* on CDs because we had an overdue commitment to Warner Brothers. Blu-ray was too expensive and cumbersome. I needed another way to get high resolution out with *Archives Vol. 2*.

We had made a deal that we'd do it on CDs with a book, and I told them we'll give them the best-sounding CDs we can make. I really wanted them to do a vinyl version of it—the recordings on vinyl accompanied by a book—but it wasn't practical. There would have been somewhere between thirty and forty vinyl records for *Vol. 2*. Honestly, it was depressing to do a CD version of it, but I owed it to Warner Brothers to give it to them, since that was what they wanted.

You can see how I've struggled over the decades with developing my archives, trying to find the right technology to use and always having ideas before the technology was there.

MEMORY

Using a website for my archive still had this one big problem and it was the music again. We couldn't figure out how to do it right and make it sound great and be convenient to use. We realized that, to play it, we were going to have to use the computer, which we would need to push to play the high-res files. A major problem was all of the computer memory that would be needed to store all the recordings. We even looked at providing a hard drive containing all my music and somehow syncing it to the website. It was unwieldy.

This time we lucked out with some technology that came along just in time to solve the problem: the high-res streaming from OraStream that we evolved into Xstream.

ALL MY MUSIC IN HI-RES

When we went online with the Neil Young Archives (NYA) at neilyoungarchives.com, I was able to provide all my music in high res, just the way it was recorded, by using this new adaptive bitrate streaming. The streaming solved all of the memory and storage requirements. It also enabled us to create Apple and Android apps where all my music can be enjoyed in high res from a phone. As far as I know, it's the first app that has been able to stream at full 192/24 yet works at all bandwidths. Of course, to hear the full quality of the music, the computers and the lion's share of the cell phones still need a high-resolution-capable DAC, but even without, the music sounds better. Recall that the DAC turns the digital files into high-res analog to drive speakers and headphones. Some LG and Samsung phones have one built in. Today, at last, there is an app to match these phones' capability: the Neil Young Archives app with Xstream by NYA. (We were told not to use "Xstream" because someone else was using it. I thought of Beats by Dr. Dre and decided to go with Xstream by NYA.)

I began developing this NYA website in 2016 with Toshi Onuki, my art director, and Hannah Johnson, my project leader, and completed it in 2018. As of today, it's still evolving with many new features being added.

The NYA team: Zeke Young, Hannah Johnson,
John O'Neill, and Liela Crosset

NYA IS MY HOME

NYA also became something much more than just a repository of my material. Because so many of my fans visit, hang around, and return so often, it lets me constantly communicate directly with them. I let them know about my new activities, albums, movies, upcoming concerts, and thoughts on current events. I do this through my own newspaper on the site, the NYA *Times-Contrarian*, where I post articles on everything from music to politics.

The NYA site has so much information that we wanted to make it appealing, comfortable, and as easy as possible to spend time there and find new things. We designed NYA with images of real analog objects I grew up with that I can relate to, such as a file cabinet, VU sound meters and toggle switches that were used on tape recorders, a keyhole, and other elements that take you back to an earlier era and make it more fun. I know it's a throwback. I am, too.

Each recording in the archives includes all the related material, such as how and where it was created, who else was a part of it, and much more. There are the typewritten lyrics, my handwritten notes, and every document I had relating to the album or song. I was able to implement my time line idea just as I had hoped. It stretches across the screen, and you can travel from album to album by date or immediately jump to a specific date. With new content all the time, it just grows and grows. We've included a foldout graphic of it in this book that's a sample of what's on the website along with the file cabinet drawer.

THE CABINET

We also created a file cabinet drawer that you see when you first come to the site. Clicking on the drawer is the gateway to all my material from 1963 to today. It's all in its highest resolution! Open the cabinet drawer. Leaf through the file folders that contain my albums, movies, and videos, and all the related notes and memorabilia. Info cards pop up when you open the album to provide even more information. When you come to an item of interest, you can easily play it with a couple of clicks.

Charley Hansen, founder of Ayre Acoustics and developer of Pono, is remembered in the clicking sound of the files moving as you explore the cabinet drawer. It's a sound taken from an Ayre amplifier's revolutionary volume control. This was added in honor of Charley, who sadly passed away on November 28, 2017, just before the site was launched.

Even though it was not completed, I announced NYA to the public on December 1, 2017. Within two days we had a half-million visitors and 130,000 people signed up to listen. We're probably setting a record for the amount of high-res music that we deliver.

Access to the site and all my content was free for almost a year. That was possible because of the strong support I got for the NYA idea from my recording company, Warner Music.

In December 2018, we began charging a small introductory fee of $1.99 per month or $19.99 per year to access *all* of the content. This was necessary as it helps defray our costs to build out, maintain, and grow the site, but certainly not all of them. We also offer free access that lets you do everything except stream the music, books, films, and videos. But you still can listen to a song of the day and album of the week.

I'm really excited and proud of this site. Hannah Johnson, daughter of Larry Johnson, my old friend who started the Archives with me, was put in charge of developing NYA. It is a monumental task and she has done a great job. Ben Johnson—Larry's son, who has taken over his company, Upstream Multimedia—also helps us out regularly. I am very fortunate. We all miss Larry every day.

The site has attracted attention from around the world and has received great acclaim, such as this excerpt of a review from the *Guardian*:

And that's why Neil Young Archives feels like a breakthrough. Here at last is an online presentation of an artist's catalogue that presents the hits and the rarities, alongside all the relevant information about every track . . . But flicking through Neil Young Archives, the possibilities for other artists beam out like headlamps. Here's the future, albeit the future of the past.[9]

THE FUTURE

Just as we did with Pono, we've been able to show the record companies and the tech industry what they can do to provide quality audio. Pono proved it was possible to make a low-cost player and create a download store that delivered the highest quality and the most enjoyable audio content ever. The biggest objection to Pono was it didn't have the convenience of streaming. So, we showed once again that there is an alternative to low-quality streaming. It's Xstream by NYA, being used right now on NYA to stream all of my music at its highest resolution, twenty-four hours a day, to my music-loving fans around the world.

NYA continues to evolve and live. I'm working on it every day, and we're adding new features all the time. I'm now streaming some of my live concerts on the site. I'm also very excited about the *NYA Times-Contrarian* newspaper, which I spend a lot of time on, perhaps living my father's dream of a newspaper life. *But the real meat is the sound.*

9   Michael Hann, "Heart of Gold: Neil Young's Online Archives Are a Revolution in Fandom," *The Guardian*, June 4, 2018, https://www.theguardian.com/music/2018/jun/04/neil-young-archives.

I also want NYA to be an example for my artist friends to show them what they can do with their music and to encourage them to develop their own archive sites. I've offered to provide the technology behind NYA to other artists to make it easier for them to create an archive with their own look and to stream in high res. I'm also working to bring music collections and recordings from others to my site.

In working on NYA for as long as I have, my goal has been to create something that was small enough to control but that would ultimately get the results that I wanted—to have my music available in high res. I am sure now we must be doing it right, because so many people tell us we are *not* doing this right!

People are saying, "You're not maximizing the number of hits you're getting." You are not doing this, you're not doing that, you're not doing all these things. I'm really not interested in doing all those things. What I'm interested in doing is *not* those things.

I hesitate to push my music down *everyone's* throats. I would like to present my music to the people who love it, so they can hear it at its best. That makes me feel good because these people supported my life and music for more than fifty years. This is payback from me to them.

If the industry picks up on the quality served at NYA, sure, that would be great. But I'm not trying to expand NYA past my own audience of music lovers. My music speaks for itself. That's why I don't want to maximize the number of hits and do the normal internet marketing tricks. We are targeting just my own music lovers and, through them, other artists. I do know there will be others who notice. A lot of artists care about the audio quality of music.

I'm interested in people having a place to go where they can listen to my music and really hear it. If I can do a good job in presenting my life's work and creations, and if the archive really provides all these things, then other artists might decide to do the same thing, each having their own big place. *Am I dreaming or what? But it would sure save the sound of their music.*

The only way I could get this out and control it and keep the quality what it is, is to do it myself. I'm not really interested in promoting my own archives or building a business around that. But this can be a model for other artists, such as Paul McCartney, with his immense catalog; Metallica, a band I love; and others. It is an "end of formats" archival music platform that artists around the world can use.

Sometimes I imagine NYA as the first step to a World Music Archives. I could see other artists beginning to adopt it. Every record company on earth could be part of the World Music Archives. There would be a WMA Universal, WMA Warner Brothers, WMA Sony, WMA Blue Note, WMA Vanguard, WMA Folkways, each with their own little place. You could go to the WMA site and subscribe to whatever music companies you would like to subscribe to, to get whatever artists' archives you want to get. Wouldn't that be nice?

My friend Marc Benioff keeps telling me it's possible to profit from doing this, and my response is that's great. I think that's fine if someone else does it. My interest is proving to the world that, for a low amount of money, you can have something like this. My goal is to make this quality available to other artists and ultimately, through them, to all their fans. The money will come from music when the technology serves the people well.

Music has been such a big part of my life that I've had to speak out a lot about how the quality has been getting so bad. I've done more than complain. I've put my name and reputation behind it and have shown that there are good solutions. I'll continue to do whatever I think will help, and I hope others will join me in this pursuit. In the last chapter, I offer my suggestions for what others can do.

Chapter 27 | Neil

WHAT NEXT?

*T*aking care of the music is something I think about every day. I'm always trying to find new ways to communicate how much music means to the world and why it's important for our survival and happiness that it be enjoyed in its full glory.

I do believe that one of the big streaming platforms is going to take the leap to adaptive bitrate Xstream by NYA or similar technology at some point. Once that happens, others will follow. They'll have to. That's the way things work. Courage and foresight from one of the big streaming companies will give you what you're entitled to. Insist on hearing *all* the music.

TO THE RECORD COMPANIES: PREPARE NOW

What you're selling is mostly crappy-sounding audio that compromises the music that made you who you used to be. You're downgrading the music so much to sell as much as you can, anywhere you can, without thinking about the future of music.

I can't blame you for not offering better-sounding music if there's nothing available to play it back on. If what everybody uses to listen to it is going to dumb it down anyway, what difference does it make?

But wait! Music on Xstream by NYA sounds better right away, no matter where you are or what device you're using. That's simply because Xstream by NYA is able to play a full high-res file. All the other services are limited to a dumbed-down file.

Spotify's desktop app, for example, is limited to 320 or 160 kbps. That's two levels of quality to choose from. On an Android, iPhone, or iPad, the Spotify mobile app has four audio quality settings: 320, 160, 96, or 24 kbps.

Xstream by NYA has *15,000* levels of quality and continuously seeks the highest-quality bandwidth allowed by your device at your current location. That's anywhere from extremely low to super-high. Good bandwidth allows all music to be heard in high res, exceeding an iPhone's capabilities for playback. Still, even with that limitation, anyone can hear the difference. It's big! (Some phones by Samsung, LG, and others can play full high resolution today, but not the iPhone. You should hear NYA on those phones.)

Try listening to one of my songs on your phone using the NYA app. Now listen to the same song through Spotify or one of the other streaming services. It doesn't matter if you are using Bluetooth speakers or whatever. The Xstream music is better sounding because Xstream by NYA is able to play a file with the closest quality to the original. Spotify is not capable of that.

It's up to you, record companies, to improve the status quo of music quality. Don't wait for the new and better phones to arrive. They are coming.

Be ready. When the change comes, your music will sound as great as it can. People will be able to *feel* the difference. You will be ready to give our *best* files to the great streaming company that makes the jump first. Do it now. Save the sound of music. Let it live.

Please stop using CD masters to make vinyl if you have the original analog tapes of legacy music. You should be making great legacy vinyl from that analog, and at the same time, you can transfer these timeless pieces of art to high-resolution digital for the next generation of streaming. It's coming. Our greatest music will be preserved and shared forever.

Remember, analog deteriorates over time. Your transfers need to be done now to be saved and ready for history. Start with your all-time top 100 albums.

It does cost to do these transfers. It's your music to take care of. Be responsible to more than your three-month bean counters! See the future.

Some of you are taking high-res masters—192 masters, which is what many digital masters are—and you're making CDs from them. You're both downsampling and interpolating to make CDs. Then you make a vinyl record from the CD and ruin it before it's ever listened to. It has no chance of sounding great, but it's vinyl, so people think it's going to sound great. It's such a rip-off. I know why you're doing it. It's easier, cheaper, and you already have a CD master. You haven't improved anything. You're just sending out shit, deceiving and fooling your music-loving customers. Shame.

Lastly, rethink your pricing. If you charged the same price for all music, more listeners would go to the better quality and you'd be doing the world a huge service. And it wouldn't cost *you* any more. Maybe $2,000 for each high-res master—$50,000 to preserve your top twenty-five albums of all time at archive quality. To share the cost, make vinyl simultaneously. I ask you to bite the bullet now and transfer your analog masters to preserve the future of music history at the highest resolution. It's your responsibility.

TO THE AUDIO EQUIPMENT COMPANIES: AIM HIGHER FOR THE FUTURE

I'd like to see you offer a pure analog line of products, low, medium, and high quality, with amps and bypassable DACs. It's very simple. Design to play directly off a phone's digital output or from its analog output. I say less is more. You should support playing high-res audio and not limit to CD quality. I'm speaking especially to you, Sonos, Apple, Amazon, Google, and others with your smart speakers. You work hard to design your speakers to sound decent, but limit what they can play with your cheap and underperforming electronics. Lenbrook, a Canadian company, has improved on Sonos with their BluOS, delivering high-res audio throughout the home and proving it can be done.

Invest in better-quality DACs and amplifiers. Divest from unneeded features that compromise your sound.

There's also an opportunity for you to create new kinds of products. Great ideas that are based on simplicity and quality sound. Make a headphone with a high-quality DAC and amplifier that plugs into your phone's data port. High-resolution-capable streaming is coming. Your customers will be ready to listen to anything. Be ready, too.

TO APPLE, GOOGLE, AND AMAZON MUSIC: OPEN THE DOOR TO GREATNESS

Why don't you help preserve the history of music in its true greatness? Make the products to reproduce it and share it with the world forever.

Offer the high-resolution and CD files on your streaming services and in your stores. You are one step away from preserving the art of recorded sound—all the music of the ages since recording began. Open the door to greatness. If you offer these common-sense solutions to the people, the music companies can provide the product and the world will rejoice again with great-sounding music, feeling it to the soul. Without you, the potential is limited.

TO THE PHONE MANUFACTURERS: LEAVE A DOOR OPEN

It's just as easy to stream great adaptive bitrate sound as it is to stream the crap we have today; probably easier, since adaptive bitrate only needs one file, not several files for different audio qualities. That's what today's old-school streaming services are forced to use with their twentieth-century technology. Make your phones so they can play all the music back. Streaming services are coming to deliver it. Some are already here. Be able to play it back or have a way to get it out to a playback device that can handle it.

Unlike camera technology, you have no consistent strategy to improve audio quality. Most of you currently use low-res DACs and limit your playback to CD quality or less. When you do focus on audio, it's often about your built-in speakers instead of what is going into them. Garbage in, garbage out.

Some of you are on the right track, building in better DACs and audio players, or allowing direct access to the digital files. That would enable absolute highest-quality *twenty-first century listening*. This quality is coming to your phone. Be able to deliver it to your music-loving consumer. You can change the world.

New phones with these capabilities would be quite amazing, letting their users drive a world-class sound system anywhere with a phone, in their headphones, houses, and cars.

Providing high-quality audio from your phone is the best way to stand apart from your competitors. Audio remains your opportunity to excel. Our NYA app and others like it can now deliver high-res audio to your customers, but we need you to free the music, so they can hear it all.

TO THE STREAMING COMPANIES:
EMBRACE THE TWENTY-FIRST CENTURY

Grow with contemporary technology. Release the music. Your products are based on technology that's about twenty years old, addressing nonexistent problems that are gone. This old approach requires your customers to make unneeded compromises in their audio quality. We've solved that all now and it's working. There's no longer any need to make compromises. We'd love you to adopt what we have done with Xstream by NYA. Whether it's our way of doing it or somebody else's way, it doesn't matter. Just be aware that the technology exists to do it and it can save the sound of music.

Adaptive bitrate streaming technology is obviously superior to anything else. It's beyond formats. It's simpler. It means that you get everything you can, all the time, wherever you are, from just one file. As the streaming market progresses, one streaming company will recognize that adaptive bitrate can set it apart, yielding a huge advantage over the competition while bringing a giant benefit to customers and giving back the gift of music to the world. Everywhere music is heard, it will sound great.

TO MUSIC LOVERS: FEED YOUR SOULS

When I started making music, it was presented on vinyl records, and the listener heard everything we created. Today, with digital music, what you are getting is less than 5 percent of what I created. If you get a CD of my music, then you hear less than 25 percent. Digital is numbers. It's all math. That's just how it adds up. You are getting a raw deal from the technology and record companies. I am sorry about that.

When I started my music career, everyone loved music and it was a big thing. It brought joy and it brought tears. Music reflected our lives and we felt it. That was when we heard it all, 100 percent of it.

You're the ones who are getting screwed the worst. You're not getting what it is you think you're getting. You are getting a small percentage of what people used to hear and feel.

Look, I don't want you to feel bad. You're probably enjoying music because it's music. Music is good, so you're going to enjoy it in almost any shape you can get it. Just recognizing the song is not enough, though. That's not a good enough reason to settle for 5 percent of the music you bought.

I want you to *feel* music. You deserve it. Music has a lot more to give to you and your soul.

Acknowledgments

Neil and Phil

We'd like to thank the many people who have helped us on this journey to improve the sound of music.

To those who were a part of Pono: the late Elliot Roberts, Craig Kallman, John Hamm, Pedram Abrari, Bruce Botnick, Mark Goldstein, Ian Kendrick, Mike Nuttall, and Bob Stuart, all of whom helped with the research for this book. Thanks to the rest of the Pono team: James Berberian, Irina Boykova, Greg Chao, Rick Cohen, Kevin Fielding, Dave Gallatin, Simon Gatrall, Damani Jackson, Sami Kamangar, Franz Krachtus, Randy Leasure, Dave Paulsen, Ariel Brown, Jason Rubenstein, Reynold Starnes, Zeke Young, Gigi Brisson, and Harvey Alison. Special thanks to the late Charley Hansen and Pegi Young.

To our PCH manufacturing team: Liam Casey, Matthieu Charlier, Eliza Choi, John Garvey, Carlos Martin, Charlie Nolan, Ray Porter, Jennie Yang, Andre Yousefi, Norman Zhu, and many more.

To those who have been a part of NYA: Hannah Johnson, Toshi Onuki, Zeke Young, Katie Fox, Liela Crosset, Frankie Tan, Kelvin Lee, John O'Neill, Stuart Mouritzen, Mike Ryan, Gordon Smith, and Scott Andrew and the Lookout Management team: Frank Gironda, Bonnie Levetin, and Tim Bruegger.

To those who have supported us the entire time and through the ups and downs with encouragement and advice: Marc Benioff, John Hanlon, John Tyson, and Dan Hesse.

A special thanks to Larry Reich and Craig Kallman for bringing us together.

Thanks also to our wives, Daryl and Jane, for their loving support.

Thanks to our agent, Bill Gladstone; our editor, Vy Tran, who did a superb job in helping us tell our story; and our copyeditor, James Fraleigh. Thanks to Glenn Yeffeth, Publisher of BenBella Books, and to the company's great support staff.

Finally, special thanks to each of the investors and to all of the others we may have omitted; the Kickstarter supporters, the Pono community, and to all of the fans who helped us along the way and believed then and still believe how important it is *to feel the music.*

About the Authors

NEIL YOUNG is one of the world's most famous musicians, with millions of followers around the globe. He's a Canadian singer-songwriter, musician, producer, director, and screenwriter. His music career began in the 1960s, when he formed Buffalo Springfield with Stephen Stills. He joined Crosby, Stills & Nash, and has recorded solo albums with his backing bands Crazy Horse and Promise of the Real. Young has recorded a steady stream of studio and live albums. He also plays piano, guitar, and harmonica on many of his albums, which frequently combine folk, rock, country, and other musical styles. He continues to tour and record new albums.

Young has received numerous Grammy and Juno awards. He's a member of the Rock & Roll Hall of Fame and is the thirty-fourth-greatest rock 'n' roll artist in *Rolling Stone* magazine's list of the 100 greatest artists of all time.

Young is an environmentalist and outspoken advocate for the welfare of small farmers, having cofounded the benefit concert Farm Aid with Willie Nelson. Young helped found The Bridge School, an educational organization for children with severe verbal and physical disabilities.

Young has appeared as a guest on many major network shows, including *The Late Show with Stephen Colbert*, *The Tonight Show Starring Jimmy Fallon*, *The Late Show with David Letterman*, *Saturday Night Live*, and *The Big Interview with Dan Rather*, and has written two previous books: *Waging Heavy Peace: A Hippie Dream* and *Special Deluxe: A Memory of Life and Cars*.

He continues to enjoy a huge following with his frequent concert tours. Young resides in Malibu, California, and Colorado, with his wife, Daryl.

PHIL BAKER has been developing consumer electronics products for his entire career, including many iconic products for Polaroid, Apple, Seiko, Barnes & Noble, Think Outside, Pono, and others. He holds more than thirty patents and was a San Diego Ernst & Young Entrepreneur of the Year for his invention of the Think Outside Stowaway Keyboard.

Baker is the author of *From Concept to Consumer*, which details the product development process and is a valuable resource for anyone wanting to embark on developing a high-tech consumer product.

Baker is also a technology writer and journalist. He wrote a weekly column, "On Technology," for the *San Diego Transcript* for twelve years and continues to write technology columns for a number of websites. He was recipient of the 2015 San Diego Columnist of the Year award.

Baker holds a BS degree in physics from Worcester Polytechnic Institute, a master's degree in engineering from Yale, and an MBA from Northeastern University.

Baker and Young began working together to develop the Pono Music Player in 2012 and continue to work together on other projects, including the Neil Young Archives. Baker resides in Solana Beach, California, with his wife, Jane.